The Family Cruise Companion's Guide to Cruising with Kids

The Family Cruise Companion's Guide to Cruising with Kids

Elaine M. Warren

ISBN: 0692885706
ISBN 13: 9780692885703

INTRODUCTION

So, you are considering taking your family on a cruise? If your family includes small children, you may have some concerns or worries about the wisdom of taking a cruise vacation. This book should help address those concerns.

I have been enjoying cruise vacations, both with and without kids, for nearly 15 years, and I am delighted to share what I have learned with you. To date, I have sailed on dozens of cruises that have covered more than 170 days at sea. This cruise history includes substantial experience traveling with small children. Nineteen of my past cruises have included at least one child under the age of 5; ten of them included at least one infant or toddler (under the age of 3). And, most of these cruises involved my own children: My oldest son sailed on his first cruise when he was an 18-month-old toddler, and my youngest child first joined us at the age of just 4 months. I have traveled on ships that were designed to be family friendly, those that merely tolerated children (as in – they should be seen and not heard), and everything in between.

Planning a cruise for your family for the first time can be overwhelming. You could spend hours mining the internet for helpful tips and advice relating to cruising while still feeling concerned that you might be missing something. Your vacation time is limited, and you want to make sure that every member of your family can enjoy it. This book should help you do that. The basic information that you need for any cruise has been collected here, as well as special tips, advice, and information pertinent to families traveling with young children. All of your important bases should be covered here.

CHAPTER 1

DECIDING TO GO ON A CRUISE (SHOULD YOU DO IT?)

A. Benefits of Cruising

The first time I went on a cruise, I was relatively young, single, and traveling on vacation with some girlfriends. Cruising had not been my idea for a vacation. I had grudgingly acquiesced to the plans of others. I was highly skeptical that I would have a good time. No one in my family had ever been on a cruise. The closest my family had ever been to cruising was catching a random episode of *The Love Boat*. I had vague recollections of a perky cruise director and a bumbling captain. What little I knew or had heard did not seem particularly appealing. And the idea of being on a boat for days on end, living out of a closet of a room with limited cheesy entertainment options, and surrounded by a predominantly geriatric crowd did not sound like fun. I simply could not imagine myself playing shuffleboard or hanging by the pool all day, every day. Nevertheless, my friends prevailed, and I schlepped on board.

Much to my surprise, I absolutely loved it. At the end of seven days, I gleefully admitted that it had been one of the best vacations I had experienced. Things I loved:

- Being on a cruise ship was like a giant floating resort. We unpacked once and woke up every day in a new place.
- We saw many different places without the burden of navigating the logistics in between—no trains, buses, or commuter flights.
- Loved the dining options – and surprisingly, loved being at a fixed table every night.
- Loved the variety of entertainment – casino, shows, dancing, and even movie options.
- Loved roaming the ship – being able to find quiet nooks to sit and read, but finding large groups to socialize with as the mood suited.
- Loved the cruise-pass concept – the convenience of one card for everything.
- Loved that most everything we needed was included in one price.

These positive factors continued when I started traveling with my family and young children. And I believe many of the same things that appealed to me will appeal to a wide range of families.

Overall, cruising provides an incredibly flexible vacation alternative. It can accommodate a wide range of travel personalities. The more independent traveler can treat the ship as a floating resort/hotel and maximize time off the ship doing self-directed activities. Active folks often have options for adventure and sports activities on larger ships – zip line, running tracks, rock climbing, surfing simulators, etc. For the more leisurely or sedentary crowd, they can enjoy numerous options for soaking up the sun, lounging by a pool, soaking in a hot tub, or sampling various spa offerings. And, all passengers can peruse a menu of shore excursions categorized by activity and exertion level, and select those that are most appealing. Or not.... Port of call visits are optional, not mandatory. Travelers can remain on-board for their entire trip, if that is what they desire.

Furthermore, cruising offers good value for your vacation dollars because the price includes all essential meals and lodging, complementary or inexpensive childcare options, and allows you to conveniently visit many destinations in a short period of time. Plus, a cruise offers a wide variety of on-board entertainment and recreational offerings to appeal to a range of interests and ages – including space to do nothing at all.

B. Should I Bring My Infant/Toddler/Small Child?

Although a cruise can be a great vacation option for families, people often express concerns about taking babies and toddlers on a cruise—as opposed to big kids and teenagers. A frequent question that pops up on various Internet message boards that I have seen is some version of: "Is it crazy to take my baby/toddler on a cruise?" The concerns expressed in the question and in some of the inevitable negative responses are fear of the reactions of other passengers and whether it is possible to have fun with kids in tow.

My short answer is – No, you are not crazy! Forget about the naysayers. You and your family can go and have a wonderful time.

It surprises me how often these types of questions receive a slew of negative responses. Notably, most of the naysayers usually have never themselves traveled on a cruise with children. Moreover, many of the objections that some folks have to cruising with kids apply generally to traveling with kids virtually anywhere. For instance, sometimes people have lamented that their baby was too young for kids club, so someone was chained to the room for nap times. This is a basic childcare issue and one that you would face at most hotels or resorts. But, more importantly, with pre-planning, it is a concern that can be addressed.

Some of the naysayers say don't bring your child because she is too young to remember it. I always find that puzzling. Unless the sole or primary purpose for this particular vacation is to benefit the baby/toddler/small child, why should the entire family have a hiatus on fun just because the smallest member won't remember how much fun was had? There are lots of fun things that families do every day that babies won't necessarily remember but we do them anyway because we want to enjoy our lives in real time, and we want the family to be there for the family activity.

When my oldest son was two years old, we went on an Alaska cruise, in part because there was an incredible sale that has never been repeated (yet). Everyone had a wonderful time, including my two-year-old. On the last night, when I told him we were leaving the cruise the next day to go home, he burst into tears and wailed "Why?!"

Fast-forward seven years: The now nine-year-old has no real recollection of visiting Alaska. He knows from the photos and souvenirs that he was there. And he also knows from the photos and various funny stories and anecdotes that his 2-year-old self had a great time. Regardless of his personal recollection of the event, he still enjoys hearing the stories.

Do I regret taking my then 2-year-old to Alaska because he no longer remembers it 7 years later? Absolutely not. I, myself, remember it quite well and cherish my own memories of that trip – some of which would likely not have occurred if I were traveling with a 9 or 10-year-old vs. a 2-year-old. The 2-year-old's look of excited wonder when first encountering a group of actual Alaskan Husky puppies playing next to the street, his overly enthusiastic participation in the simulated gold mining excursion, and his attempts to converse with a bald eagle.

If it is an activity that other family members will enjoy, doesn't it make sense to enjoy the opportunity now when it is available? Who knows whether you will be in a position to do it at some unspecified "right time" in the future. And if it is something that you really enjoy, you can do it again.

Other common objections or concerns involve the possibility of negative reactions from other passengers to the presence of small children. But, if you select your cruise well, this hypothetical reaction should not be a concern. If you choose a family-oriented cruise, there will be many other small children on board. The addition of your brood will not meaningfully change the tenor of the cruise for other passengers. (By way of example, on one of our recent holiday cruises, it was announced that 1700 of the approximately 3700 passengers sailing were children.) People who truly do not want to be around children either avoid such cruises or they have an option to spend most of their time in the adults-only portions of the ship.

So, bottom line, should you take your baby/toddler on a cruise with you? If you have a built-in attractive alternative – for instance, you can leave your child with excited grandparents/relatives – that's great. But fear that you are making a mistake should not be the motivating factor in your decision.

C. Reality Check: Babies are Special

Obviously, cruising will not be a good choice for every family. Cruising with small children does present challenges. But most of those challenges are all of the same ones that you would have on any travel vacation – *e.g.*, navigating naps, tantrums, picky eaters, etc.

Although cruising overall offers good value, you may find it annoying to have to pay full price for your baby or toddler. Usually, there is no discount for kids, even though they eat much less than an adult. Or, in the case of babies, they may not be eating the cruise line food at all. That said, the price for the 3rd and 4th passenger in a room is typically substantially less than the fare for the first two passengers—regardless of age. At times you may be able to catch a special promotion that results in a discount for child passengers – e.g., kids sail free promotions; 2nd passenger for 50% off.

You will also have to pack substantially more items if you are traveling with a baby or toddler than you would otherwise. Most things must be brought on board. You cannot reliably expect to buy anything that you truly need on the ship; either they don't carry it, or they may run out quickly. Do not be afraid to pack excess diapers or formula. You don't want to run out in the middle of the ocean with one or two sea days between you and a store.

Finally, your childcare options for babies and toddlers will most likely be more limited than what is available for children over the age of 3. But you still have options, and with solid research and planning, you can find a cruise that will accommodate your family's needs. See Chapter 7 on Childcare Issues.

SELECTING A CRUISE

As soon as you start perusing cruise options for your family, you will see that there are scores, if not hundreds, of potentially viable options. Trying to assess all of the options and make a decision can be daunting and overwhelming. Resolving a few threshold issues can help you evaluate and narrow down your options. Some key questions include: Will you use a travel agent or make independent arrangements? What requirements do you have for an itinerary (in terms of scheduling, duration, geography, and price)? Once you have those basics nailed down, you can assess whether certain cruise lines have characteristics that will better meet your family's needs, and also determine what type of stateroom you require. The information presented below will help you assess these issues.

A. Do you need a travel agent?

These days, you can make almost all of your family vacation plans online cheaply and efficiently using websites like *Orbitz, Tripadvisor,* and *Expedia.* But when it comes to planning a cruise vacation, this may be an instance where you will want to depart from your usual approach and consider getting assistance from a travel agent.

According to industry trade publications, approximately 70% of cruisers work with an agent when booking their trip. And there are many good reasons for that. I have booked a couple of cruises directly with the cruise line, but the vast majority of my cruises have been booked using agents. Based on my personal experience, I see the following benefits in using a travel agent for booking cruises: (i) access to an agent's superior knowledge and experience; (ii) eligibility for additional promotions and savings; and (iii) making better use of my own personal time.

Unlike some of your other family travel, booking a cruise on your own without agent assistance will not save you either time or money, and you may well miss out on some promotional perks that would add additional value to your trip.

(i) Agent vs. direct booking

For purposes of this discussion, I am comparing booking with a travel agent with booking directly with a cruise line – either through its online reservation system or through its website.

Booking through a travel agent can help you plan a better trip because you can make more informed decisions about available options. (This, of course, assumes that you have a good agent. See below for a discussion on how to find a good agent.) A knowledgeable and experienced travel agent can help sort out the various room categories and the related amenities; provide guidance on parts of the ship likely to be noisy, crowded, rocky, etc.; and provide current feedback regarding various cruise lines or specific ships (based on their own experience and recent reports from other clients). Moreover, travel agents are repeat players, so they are more likely to know the questions to ask or requests to make that you would not think of and the reservation agent is not in a position to volunteer. They will also have better knowledge of and access to potential upgrades.

You will not be charged for using the services of a travel agent. While it is true that the travel agencies make their money through commissions, the cruise lines pay those commissions, not the passengers.

Furthermore, booking through a travel agent can help you save money, and can also help increase the overall value of your trip in other ways. First, many agents offer supplemental promotional benefits such as: additional on-board credit; pre-paid gratuities; free dinners at specialty restaurants; a bottle of champagne; and complementary airport transfers.

The travel agent, too, will usually stack their promotional benefits on top of whatever promotions the cruise line happens to be running. My personal favorite is frequent flier miles. And there are often special promotions involving mile multipliers of 4X, 6X or more. Many times, I have been able to accrue 30,000 to 60,000 miles via a cruise promotion.

Second, the cruise lines often change the prices of various sailings and are constantly offering a variety of promotions. The cruise line will not, however, automatically give you the benefit of a subsequent sale price. An agent can help you track that and request that any new credits or promotions be applied. This last point cannot be overstated, particularly if you book far in advance. There have been numerous times where I have run across an ad promotion that seemed applicable to a sailing that I booked several months prior, contacted my travel agent, and she was able to have the new discount or benefits applied immediately.

Booking through a travel agent can also help you save time (and minimize your personal frustration). When you call the reservation line for a cruise line directly, there is often a long wait time to get a response from a live reservation agent (*e.g.*, 20-30 minutes). Sometimes, during peak times, wait times can be an hour or more. If you have an agent, it is your agent on the phone waiting, not you. He or she will simply get back to you with the ultimate response. There have been numerous times when we have had to circle back with a cruise line. It is extremely beneficial not to have to spend my own time on hold all those times (examples – new advertised promotion and we want to see if we can take advantage of the sale to get better pricing (in the U.S. this is allowed); wanting to change stateroom assignments if better ones have opened up; booking certain add-ons.) Sometimes you can get a better answer from the cruise line if you call back to speak with someone else, or call back to speak with a supervisor. An agent can make all of those follow-up calls and also knows when it is likely fruitful to continue to press or follow-up on an issue.

Likewise, if you are calling the reservation line directly, you will likely get a different person each time. By working with an agent, you have the benefit of having one contact person who already knows your backstory rather than getting a new person every time you call back.

Some people have the misperception that avoiding a travel agent will save them money. In the context of booking a cruise, this is simply not true. You are unlikely to save money by making your reservations independently. And you may miss out on the opportunity to take advantage of subsequent fare drops and sales. Cruise lines do not provide any additional incentives for booking directly with them. In fact, when you book on board through future cruises – or when they send direct mail ads – they always make a special point of giving a call out to your travel agent. Cruise lines are not looking to undercut travel agents.

When can it be a disadvantage to use a travel agent? One potential disadvantage that I have found is that you cannot contact the cruise line directly about most aspects of your reservation pre-departure if you booked through a travel agent. So, for instance, if you want to make a payment, you will be directed to do so through your agent. If you have a question about your specific reservation, you will also be referred back to the agent who booked you. One way to think of it is that the cruise line is paying a commission to the agent. It wants to get full value for its payment. But if you are working with a good agent— someone who is responsive and easy to communicate with—this really should not be a true problem. When I have any issues, questions or concerns, I email my agent, and she takes care of the follow-up.

(2) How to select a travel agent

If you decide to use a travel agent, you should work with an agent who specializes in cruises. They are extremely knowledgeable about every aspect of your trip and can make informed suggestions. For example, they can provide:

- insights into more family friendly ships or itineraries;
- information on cruise lines that are a better fit for your travel party;
- information on cruises that may be a poor fit for your travel party (e.g., ones that may be magnets for spring break partiers);
- advice about booking Caribbean cruises during hurricane season;
- assistance in placing the dozens of different types and categories of stateroom options in perspective.

So how do you find a good cruise specialist? As with most things in life, a personal referral is usually a great place to start. Do you know someone who has cruised before or who cruises often? Ask them for a personal contact. I used several different agents for my first few cruises, each of whom I met through various credit card or frequent flier promotions. Through one of those same routes, I met my current travel agent who provided such phenomenal service that she earned my loyalty. I subsequently booked my next dozen cruises with her, and she is always the first person I contact when I am planning a cruise vacation.

If you do not have a personal referral, other places to look include membership or affinity groups with whom you have relationships, or your favorite frequent flier or frequent travel program. Some examples of airlines and other partners that offer their own cruise promotions: *American Airlines, Delta Airlines, United Airlines, Spirit Airlines, Jet Blue Airways, Marriott Rewards, Hilton Hotels, Choice Hotels*. It is worth noting that, in most instances, each of these companies is not actually fielding its own private team of travel agents. While the booking will be branded under their particular travel program, these brands will often have partnerships with a large travel agent network that will provide the actual agents to do the legwork. *World Travel Holdings* (WTH), for instance, operates the travel program for most major airlines, several hotel companies, a large wholesale club, and other large travel programs.

Most major airlines now offer their own branded travel program. When you book through an agent affiliated with that airline, there will be additional perks associated with the booking. For instance, *United Cruises* often has promotions in which you earn 6x to 10x miles on *United Airlines* for the money spent on the cruise if booked through their branded agent. Those agents are still able to offer the promotions advertised by specific cruise lines that you see around. So, for instance, if a cruise line were offering a two-sail-for-the-price-of-1 promotion, you would still get the benefit of that promotional pricing in addition to the bonus airline miles. Some credit cards, as well, have affiliations with agents, and if you use those agents, you can earn some benefit attributable to the card.

If you participate at a significant level in any airline, hotel or other programs, you should check whether they offer travel agent services and whether there are special promotions available for booking through their program.

When looking at promotions offered by travel partners or credit card companies, you should compare across programs. The companies do not necessarily offer promotions that are equally valuable.

By way of example, in one instance of planning a particular cruise, I had a high frequent flier status with Airline A, and I also had a separate premium credit card with an unrelated credit card company that offered travel benefits and reward points. My travel companion had a high frequent flier status with a competing airline. She also had a branded credit card affiliated with that same airline. For one particular cruise that we wanted to book (for illustration purposes, assume $7500 for a balcony room for 4 people), we determined that if I booked using my special credit card travel service, I would get the benefit of 10,000 bonus points. (So 7500 points for the price of the cruise + 10,000 bonus points = 17,500 points for the cruise.) A second option involved booking through the travel service of my then-preferred airline (Airline A). For using Airline A's travel service, I would receive double miles based on the price of the cruise, and an additional double miles if I also used the credit card affiliated with that airline. (So 7500 x 4 = 30,000 miles on Airline A). But if I chose a third option of using the travel service of my friend's preferred airline (Airline B), it had a promotion that awarded 4X bonus miles for booking the cruise with its service, and had an enhanced award of 6X bonus miles if you booked at a balcony level or higher. Plus, you earned double miles for using the credit card branded with that airline. (So our $7500 balcony cabin would earn 7500 x 8 = 60,000 miles on Airline B.) For people who care about miles, this is obviously a significant difference.

When you are consulting with a prospective agent, find out whether she has firsthand experience with the brands/ships that interest you. A true cruise specialist has actually been onboard various ships and can provide firsthand advice about the different options available. You should expect something more than the ability to read and summarize from cruise line documentation.

Some basic questions to ask when vetting an agent: Can he or she explain the differences between different cruise lines? How many cruises has she taken in the past 1 or 2 years? How many cruises total has she taken? Does she have any industry certifications? Find out with which cruise lines she has previously cruised.

Finally, you can also search for agents in your area on the websites of relevant professional organizations such as the *American Society of Travel Agents* (ASTA) (focus on cruise specialists) or *Cruise Lines International Association* (CLIA). CLIA is a global cruise industry trade association. Please note that most professional agents have the ability to be members of CLIA. However, CLIA also offers certifications that impose substantive requirements. They have several different levels of certification that require increasing levels of professional experience and training. Each of the different levels requires that the agent has participated in a certain number of ship inspections and has personally taken a certain number and type of cruises. So, for instance, one of the highest classifications requires that the agent has participated in six ship inspections and personally sailed on two cruises that were at least 2 or more nights, at least 2 cruises that were at least 7 or more nights, and at least 1 cruise that was 10 or more nights. Moreover, the qualifying cruises must be from different geographic regions (e.g., Caribbean, Mediterranean, Alaska). Note, however, that none of these formal certifications are required to be a good travel agent. But this does provide you, the consumer, a yardstick for evaluating the experience level of a prospective agent.

B. Selecting An Itinerary - Factors to consider

The quickest way to start narrowing your pool of potential cruise options is to choose a general itinerary. Several factors will guide your decisions: when you want to go; where you want to leave from; where you want to go; how long you want to go; and how much you are willing to pay for it.

I will provide a brief overview of how each of these factors can influence your itinerary selection.

(i) Time of year

Cruising for certain parts of the world can be very seasonal, so if you are limited to a certain time window (*e.g.*, you are restricted to a certain time of year because of school/holiday schedules), and/or if you have your heart set on visiting certain places, this will influence the range of options available to you.

Stated broadly, you can generally sail Caribbean, Australian, and Hawaiian itineraries year-round. For the Caribbean, peak season runs December through April. Hurricane season runs June through November (with most storms concentrated in August, September, and October). Australia is also a year-round cruise destination. You should remember, however, that their seasons run the opposite of the seasons in North America. So, for instance, a Christmas Holiday cruise will be "summer" weather in Australia. For Hawaii, while you have year-round options for sailings, only Norwegian Cruise Line offers sailings during the summer. High season for Hawaii runs from late December through April.

For Mediterranean itineraries and Alaskan itineraries, the bulk of options will be available in the spring and summer. The Alaskan cruise season runs May to September. High season runs June through August. And while there are some instances of year-round options in the Mediterranean, most sailings run spring through fall. For those families that are constrained by school schedules, all of the foregoing itineraries could be viable options for summer break.

Notable itineraries that are largely unavailable in the summer are the Panama Canal, Central America, and South America. Also, options for Far East Asia and Southeast Asia can be very limited. For the Panama Canal, the season runs October to April. For South America, the season runs November to early May. Most Asian itineraries run November through May.

(2) Desired Departure/Return Port

The cruise lines have established numerous departure ports across the United States. Thus, families have many options from which to choose. This can play an important role in budgeting and planning, depending on how far or novel the selected port is from your home city. You can gain substantial savings on your cruise vacation by choosing a location close to home that is drivable or otherwise accessible by a cheap flight. Alternatively, you can select a more distant departure city and build a few extra vacation days around it.

Similar to the relationship between various airports and major airlines, not all cruise lines embark from all ports. Particular cruise lines dominate some ports. For instance, currently, only *Royal Caribbean* and *Celebrity* depart from Cape Liberty, New Jersey. The dominant line in Galveston is *Carnival*.

Many ports have cruises leaving for the Caribbean, *e.g.*, New Jersey, Baltimore, Galveston, and New Orleans. But if you want to maximize the available options – your best starting point is Florida, which has five different ports. Every major cruise line has at least one ship departing from a Florida port:

- Fort Lauderdale-Port Everglades (*Carnival, Celebrity, Holland America, Princess, Royal Caribbean, Seabourn Cruises, Silversea*)
- Jacksonville (*Carnival*)
- Miami (*Azamara, Carnival, Celebrity, Crystal Cruises, Disney, MSC Divina, Norwegian, Oceania, Regent Seven Seas, Royal Caribbean*)
- Port Canaveral (*Carnival, Disney, Norwegian, Royal Caribbean*)
- Tampa (*Carnival, Norwegian, Holland America, Royal Caribbean*)

There are also several ships from different cruise lines sailing from each of the following ports:

- Baltimore, Maryland (*Carnival* and *Royal Caribbean*)
- Bayonne, New Jersey (*Royal Caribbean* and *Celebrity*)
- Boston, Massachusetts (*Holland America, Norwegian, Royal Caribbean*)
- Galveston, Texas (*Disney, Carnival,* and *Royal Caribbean*)
- Los Angeles, California (*Carnival, Crystal Cruises, Cunard, Norwegian, Oceania, Princess, Royal Caribbean, Silversea*)
- New Orleans, Louisiana (*Carnival, Norwegian, Royal Caribbean*)

- New York, New York (*Carnival, Crystal, Cunard, Holland America, MSC Cruises, Norwegian, Oceania, Princess, Regent Seven Seas* and *Silversea*)
- San Diego, California (*Celebrity, Disney, Holland America, Norwegian*)
- San Francisco, California (*Celebrity, Cunard, Oceania, Princess, Regent Seven Seas*)
- Seattle, Washington (*Carnival, Celebrity, Holland America, Norwegian, Princess,* and *Royal Caribbean*).

Finally, with the exception of some river cruises (out of Charleston), there are a handful of ports that feature solely (for now) *Carnival* cruises: Charleston, South Carolina; Jacksonville, Florida; Mobile, Alabama; and Norfolk, Virginia.

Outside of North America, there are also ports across the world for more adventurous travel. For instance, many Mediterranean cruises depart from Barcelona, Rome (Civitavecchia), and Venice; Asia cruises depart from major cities such as Hong Kong, Singapore, and Tokyo; and Australia/New Zealand cruises depart from Sydney, Auckland, Melbourne, Brisbane, and Perth.

(3) Length of cruise

How much time do you have to vacation? Is there a school calendar to work around? I personally believe that a good starting point is the standard 7-day itinerary, particularly if you have never cruised. Seven days is sufficient time to see a few ports, experience a couple of sea days, and gain meaningful exposure to cruising as a vacation. Something less than 7 days does not really give you the full flavor of the cruising experience, but if you are cautious about this new experience, there are also options for 3 and 4 day cruises. Keep in mind, however, that the nicer and newer ships will be sailing the longer itineraries.

(4) Number of port days vs. sea days

Other points to consider are the number of port days vs. sea days and whether there are any "overnights" in port. The actual ports visited will have their obvious appeal (or not), but there is also much to love about sea days. They are an opportunity to truly just be. No schedule to worry about at all unless you really want an agenda. No tour. No bus. No worry about getting back to the ship. Undoubtedly, you may want to do some strategizing around the potential crowd aspect – because now every single passenger and every single crewmember is actually truly confined to one space. So, for instance, there will be lots of people at the pool, and you will want to plan for spa appointments or the like early.

Some itineraries may also include an "overnight" stay in port. This is often at the beginning or end of a cruise, but more cruises are now including overnights in intermediate ports. So for instance, a recent *Celebrity* cruise in Asia involved 4 overnights in a 14-day itinerary; several Mediterranean itineraries involve 2 overnights. This gives you the opportunity to explore more of the city and surrounding environs while still having a place to sleep.

(5) Budget

The amount of money that you have available to spend on a family vacation obviously plays a big role in deciding which cruise to purchase. Here are some general strategies to consider when trying to maximize the stretch of your vacation dollars:

(a) *Select a nearby departure port.*

If you are working with a limited or less flexible budget, the first factor to consider is your departure port. Consider driving to a port that is relatively nearby – a day's drive or less. According to industry trade groups, there are cruise ports within driving distance of 75% of North American vacationers. You can drive on the day of embarkation and park at the port. The savings in airfare and hotel should be substantial.

(b) *Book very early and/or during sales season.*

If you are looking for the best deals, you should try to book early – as in 9-12 months or more in advance. These are usually the best rates available, and you can continue to benefit from any additional price drops or promotions that occur later in the year.

You should also look at options during "Wave Season," which runs from January through March. During this period, cruise lines present their most aggressive offers for the upcoming year. These are promotions that are available for sailings throughout the year, but the special discounts and perks accrue for booking during the wave season and placing a deposit. Deposits are typically refundable with timely cancellation notice. Sample promotions: Buy one get one free; Kids sail free; selection of 2 or 3 complementary perks such as an unlimited beverage package and prepaid gratuities.

Another strategy is to book sailings during non-peak times when school is in session. Of course, this strategy will typically not work well if you actually have school age children that you want to take with you.

(c) Be flexible as to cabin selection.

If you are flexible and not particular about type or location of your cabin, last minute bookings can yield great savings. In this instance, last minute means three to six weeks out. This will typically be around the final payment deadline, and the cruise line will know how many vacancies remain to be filled. Similarly, you can save money by booking a "guarantee" room instead of a specific cabin. You will be guaranteed a cabin within a certain category or higher. Thus, you have the potential for a last minute upgrade. But, you also have the potential of being assigned to the worst possible option in the category you selected. Nor do you have any control over the location on the ship that you are assigned. Thus, you could potentially be placed in a noisy or high-traffic area that you would prefer to avoid.

(d) Consider alternative room configurations.

Consider whether alternative room configurations will work for you, and have your travel agent price out various options. For instance, getting two connecting balcony staterooms instead of an expensive suite. Likewise, getting a balcony room with an adjacent inside room. Depending on the make-up of your travel party, this last option could be quite attractive. In many instances, the price of a balcony for two persons and an indoor cabin for two persons is only a few hundred dollars more than a balcony for four people; and, you end up with almost twice the living space and an additional bathroom.

(e) Select an older ship.
Investigate itineraries on older ships. Cruises on older ships are usually much cheaper than the sailings on whatever the latest addition to the cruise line fleet happens to be. Many times these older ships have been recently refurbished or upgraded and can provide great value. So, for instance, *Royal Caribbean's Adventure of the Seas* (the first cruise ship I ever sailed on) first sailed in 2001. It was subsequently re-furbished in 2009, and then it was again upgraded in 2016. The 2016 upgrades include the addition of a new waterpark complete with water slides, a new two-story golf course, and a flowrider surf simulator. Upgraded specialty restaurants have also been added. These are amenities comparable to ones found on the newer Oasis class of ships, but without the Oasis class pricing.

(f) Plan ahead while still on-board.
Finally, once you are on-board, you should consider booking another cruise for next year. Some of the best deals available are offered on-board the ship to repeat customers. These deals often include reduced deposits – or essentially free

deposits, fare discounts, and on-board credit that could be available immediately (as in on the current cruise). You are not locked into a specific itinerary or time window, and you can freely change your plans later. The booking can also be transferred to your favorite travel agent.

(6) Geography

You have multiple options to choose from when considering geography. Looking for relaxing beach escape? Culture and art? More focused on the resort aspect than any particular destination? There is some destination to fit almost every taste. Popular regions include the Caribbean, Alaska, the Mediterranean, Hawaii, South/Central America, Asia, and Australia/New Zealand/ South Pacific. Certain regions tend to receive longer itinerary schedules than others. South America cruises are often 12-14 days or more. Meanwhile, you can find Caribbean cruises as short as 3 or 4 days.

I could not begin to summarize or even identify all the different places in the world that you can visit by cruise ship. Instead, I will say a few words about some popular destinations, and share some thoughts on evaluating others.

(a) *Most Popular Itineraries for North American Travelers*

(i) Caribbean

According to CLIA, the industry trade group, the Caribbean (including the Bahamas) is the number one destination for cruisers – attracting more than 35% of travelers. You can book a Caribbean cruise at virtually any time of the year. And there is a wide range of itineraries from 3 or 4 days to 14 days or more (using back-to-back sailings, which some people love). If the Caribbean appeals to you, you will have a wide range of ships and cruise lines, and a wide range of price points from which to choose. The Caribbean generally is a very accessible location. It is a great option for first time cruisers, and for families traveling with small children.

A downside of choosing a Caribbean itinerary is that some ports will be extremely crowded at certain times of the year. There can be 3, 4 or 5 ships docked on the same day – collectively disembarking 10,000 passengers to visit the shops, sites, and complicating traffic. You should also be mindful that many times itineraries change during hurricane season. Sometimes these changes are announced in advance (close to departure), but sometimes changes are made after you have already started sailing.

Ships depart for the Caribbean from numerous destinations throughout the U.S., so it should be relatively easy to find something that will accommodate your schedule and budget. In addition to various ports in Florida – Fort Lauderdale, Miami, Port Canaveral – major cruise lines depart for the Caribbean from Galveston, New Orleans, Baltimore, and Newark. Generally, the newer ships depart from Florida. Be aware that the farther your starting point is away from the islands, the more sea days you will have because the ship has to get there and back. So, for instance, ships leaving from Newark will often start with two back-to-back sea days.

Caribbean cruise itineraries generally fall into three categories: Eastern, Western, and Southern. They break out roughly in the following ways:

The **Eastern Caribbean** has the largest number of departure port options. It sees cruises departing from Florida, Puerto Rico, and several other ports along the Eastern seaboard. Eastern itineraries commonly include ports in the U.S. Virgin Islands, the British Virgin Islands, St. Martin/St. Maarten, Puerto Rico, Grand Turk, St. Bart's, Antigua, Anguilla, and Dominica. Eastern Caribbean itineraries will also often feature a stop at a private island (see below).

The **Western Caribbean** itineraries can be reached from the Florida ports, as well as New Orleans and Galveston. Western itineraries commonly include Cozumel, Grand Cayman, Jamaica, Honduras, and Belize.

The **Southern Caribbean** itineraries have ports that require more travel time to navigate. Thus, these cruises tend to be longer in duration. Also, the primary U.S. departure port is San Juan, Puerto Rico. Ships also depart from Barbados and St. Martin. Ports on the Southern itineraries commonly include Aruba, Bonaire, Curacao, St. Lucia, Barbados, Grenada, and Grenadines.

So which is better? If you have not previously spent much time in the Caribbean, then you can probably use ship identity and price as the deciding factors. Obviously, the individual Caribbean islands are not wholly interchangeable, but the levels of potential joys are equally great. Some islands may have white sand, while others may have black or pink sand. Some are known for particular activities like scuba diving or windsurfing, while others may have unique cultural attractions. Notwithstanding all of the many variables, the overall level of joy to be gained from a week in the Caribbean will be comparable across itineraries for most families. In other words, don't over-think the geography unless you have a specific reason to visit a specific island.

A word about *private islands*. Most of the major lines have their own private islands: *Holland America's Half Moon Cay; Disney's Castaway Cay; Princess's Princess Cays; Norwegian's Great Stirrup Cay* and *Harvest Cay; Celebrity's* and *Royal Caribbean's Cococay* and *Labadee.* Except for *Labadee* and *Harvest Cay,* all of the private islands are in the Bahamas. *Labadee* is in Haiti, and *Harvest Cay* (which is the newest cruise line island) is off the coast of Belize.

These private islands and resorts are quite nice with beautiful beaches and numerous diverse activities. However, when evaluating itineraries, you should note whether a particular stop is a private island, rather than an actual city. To the extent you are trying to absorb some of the local culture, you won't find it on the cruise line's private island. So for instance, *Royal Caribbean* has a fabulous private resort area in Haiti, *Labadee,* which I have visited many times. Although it is absolutely wonderful, I would not represent to myself or anyone else that I have actually experienced Haiti. It was literally a private playground.

Elaine M. Warren

(ii) Mediterranean/Europe

A Mediterranean cruise can be a uniquely enriching cultural experience where you and your family have the opportunity to sample a wide range of "bucket list" experiences. It is an obvious understatement to say that Europe is filled with incomparable art, culture, and history. A cruise ship can be a very convenient and efficient way to travel through Europe with small children in tow. It is on these itineraries that having a floating hotel resort as a base can considerably reduce your travel stressors – no trains, no internal flights, no noticeable passport or customs issues.

One of the biggest downsides, however, is that it can be much more expensive to cruise Europe, particularly in the peak summer months. First, you have to get there. A ticket to Barcelona or Venice will be substantially more expensive than a ticket to Florida. Air tickets for 3 or 4 people to Europe during the summer can get pretty expensive fairly quickly. Even if you are fortunate enough to have access to frequent flier tickets, the mileage awards will often come with some type of premium. Moreover, prices within Europe are generally more expensive than in the Caribbean, and this can be exacerbated by currency exchange rates.

To get the most out of this trip, you should take care to research and plan your shore excursions in advance. You should be particularly mindful that some ports can be quite a distance from the actual cities you would like to visit. For instance, cruise ships dock at Civitavecchia, which is about an hour from Rome. Similarly, the port at Livorno is about an hour and a half from Florence.

You should also not feel constrained to look only at shore excursions offered by the cruise line. With advance planning, you can often find or arrange more personalized excursions that are tailored to your needs for similar or better pricing. Also, if you are traveling with small children, having a more flexible plan can be invaluable. So, for instance, depending on the size of your travel party, or your ability to coordinate with another family, you could arrange for a large private van with an English-speaking tour guide who will take you to the sites or activities that are best suited for your group, and you can more easily take breaks or detours as needed. (For more information on planning independent excursions, see Chapter 4.)

(iii) Alaska

Alaska is another popular bucket list destination that provides an opportunity for a great cruise itinerary. More than half of the visitors to Alaska arrive by cruise ship. In recent years, an Alaska cruise has rivaled—and at times surpassed—Las Vegas as the top domestic vacation.

Alaska, which is often referred to as the last great frontier, is a very large territory dominated by thousands of acres of untamed wilderness and a smattering of cities/towns. Some towns can only be easily reached by the water. The massive glaciers and stunning marine wildlife provide a unique backdrop for a family cruise. The natural wildlife both in sea and on land is its own attraction – humpback whales, Orcas, sea otters, seals, sea lions, wild salmon, moose, grizzly and polar bears, as well as the largest population of bald eagles in the country. Many outdoor adventures can be found: stunning mountain hikes, dog sledding, fishing, kayaking, and various helicopter excursions only scratch the surface of what's available.

Alaska is most often associated with the cold snow and ice – and pictures of icy glaciers and snowcapped mountains readily come to mind. Thus, I was surprised to see vast tracts of acres of very green pine trees. Amazing natural beauty is on display every day.

The Alaska Cruise season runs from May through September. Everything shuts down on a certain date because of weather and habitability issues. There are two primary routes: the "Inside Passage," which usually runs round-trip from either Seattle or Vancouver; and the "Cross-the-Gulf" itinerary, which involves starting or ending in Anchorage from either Seward or Whittier.

Although Alaska cruises seem to be dominated by older retired couples, these cruises are also popular with multigenerational cruisers. Alaska offers much to appeal to small children. We did this cruise when my oldest son was two-years-old. As I mentioned earlier, this was the cruise where my son burst into tears wailing "Why?!" when informed that the cruise was soon ending. He really loved this cruise.

(b) More Exotic Itineraries
The itineraries discussed above generally represent the mainstream in family cruising. There are numerous other ports around the globe that can be visited by cruise ship

and they offer a gamut of varied experiences. Other areas of the world that host numerous sailings throughout the year include Hawaii, the Panama Canal and Central America, South America, Antarctica, Mexican Riviera, Canada & New England, Canary Islands, Australia/New Zealand, the South Pacific, numerous countries throughout Asia, Africa, and the Middle East.

Finally, when traveling to these international destinations, you should make sure to do your own research regarding visa requirements. Do not assume that the cruise line will be obvious or clear about visa requirements or related information.

As an example, on a cruise that originated in Asia, we learned late in the process that one country on the itinerary required Americans to have visas. Notably, we first learned this from a source other than the cruise line. After additional inquiry, we learned that it was possible to get a visa on our own through a complicated process, or we could obtain them through a convenient third party service by paying increased fees, including a specific service that was recommended by the cruise line. We opted for the cruise line endorsed third party service, and jumped through numerous hoops to get visas for four people at a substantial price tag (several hundred dollars each). Imagine my surprise and dismay when, during the embarkation process, I learned— for the first time— that it was possible to do a "group" visa through the cruise ship and the charge was $10 per person. My consternation was multiplied when I discovered that a charge for the group visas had been added to our cruise accounts. When I complained, I was told that since I had not presented the visa at embarkation – which was seven days before we reached the country at issue – I had automatically been included in the group visa. Notably, there was no indication or inquiry made when we checked in.

C. Selecting a cruise line/ship

I have set out some key information about the more family-friendly cruise lines and ships below. But you are the best judge of what types of personalities, environments, and activities will be best suited to your personal crew. Thus, once you have compiled a manageable list of potentially suitable options, you should conduct some independent research before making your final selection.

For families traveling with infants or toddlers, you should pay special attention to any restrictions on the ages of passengers. These restrictions vary across the different lines and different itineraries. Some cruise lines require a minimum of 12 months for all itineraries; some will allow children as young as 6 months on certain itineraries. For many years, *Disney* was an outlier and allowed babies as young as 12 weeks of age to board (which is why my youngest son was able to go on his first cruise), but that policy changed in 2015. Generally, cruises that involve long itineraries with many sea days will have higher age restrictions. A typical Caribbean itinerary is more likely to have a lower restriction.

You should also be aware that most cruise lines have rules about pregnant women traveling. Most lines will not allow women who will be in their third trimester of pregnancy to travel. Some lines discourage women who are less than 12 weeks into their pregnancy from traveling. Many lines also have specific requirements regarding a travel letter from your physician or similar documentation. You should check on the individual policies of the lines that apply to you.

(i) Finding a "family friendly" cruise

What makes a particular cruise family-friendly? At bottom, it is a ship that has features and programming designed to enhance the vacation experience of folks traveling with their kids. It is a ship that truly welcomes and seeks out families as opposed to simply tolerating or accommodating them. Some things to look for: Are there age appropriate activities available for everyone? Are there attractive childcare options and opportunities for some adult-only time? Are there activities geared for the whole family to enjoy together? Are there other features that make life easier for families?

If you review the numerous travel publications and blogs available, you will find a consensus view as to the most family-friendly cruises: *Disney*, *Royal Caribbean*, *Carnival*, and *Norwegian* (NCL). High marks often also go to *Celebrity*, *Holland America*, and *Princess*. (Focusing on U.S.-based market.)

When researching your cruise options, a good place to start is by assessing the kids' club options and kids' programming available on-board. Most kid programs start at age 3, and some start as early as 2. Generally, the primary kids' club will offer free programming during the daytime and early evening. The cruise lines have varying policies as to what extent kids' club is available on port days, and whether parents may leave their children on-board while they leave the ship.

Apart from the primary daytime offerings, these are some other issues to think about:

Late-night babysitting. For the late evening hours (*e.g.*, after 10:00 p.m.), there will generally be some type of group activities and/or group babysitting for a charge. If you believe that you will want to be utilizing these options frequently, you should check early whether there are any packages available. Sometimes there are kids' club packages that can be purchased which include evening babysitting, some special tours, a backpack/knapsack, and other amenities. Most lines offer group childcare in lieu of in-cabin babysitting. *Royal Caribbean* and *Celebrity*, however, offer private babysitting in staterooms at an hourly fee.

Infants & Toddlers. For younger children, there will usually be some area or playtime where younger children can go if they are accompanied by a caregiver. Both *Disney* and *Royal Caribbean* (on certain ships) have drop-off nursery options available for infants and toddlers under age three (for an additional fee). *Norwegian* now offers a drop-off nursery on one of its ships – the *Escape*.

Typically, for the nursery programs, the adult checking in the child will be provided with a pager or other communication device so that the nursery can reach them if needed. Some cruises also issue communication devices upon request for younger children in the main kids' club.

Tweens/Teens. Many ships also offer special programming or facilities for older children – tweens and teens. Many ships offer tween and teen clubs with video games, music, and dance parties. The level of adult supervision and direction as to older children varies across the cruise lines.

Character Promotions & Tie-Ins. Also, for kids' programming, certain cruise lines have various character tie-ins and character opportunities. On such cruises, there will usually be a breakfast option that can be reserved where characters participate (sometimes for a fee). There will often be numerous opportunities throughout the ship to meet the various characters and take photos. There may be parades and other character-related entertainment. Some characters will also make appearances at kids' club activities.

As of 2017, these are the most well-known character tie-ins:

- *Disney* – Numerous beloved Disney characters such as Mickey and Minnie Mouse. Phineas and Ferb. Elsa and Anna from *Frozen*. Marvel Superheroes. Various Disney princesses. *Star Wars* Day at Sea.
- *Royal Caribbean*—Main characters from popular DreamWorks movies such as the main characters from *Shrek, Kung Fu Panda, Madagascar, How to Train Your Dragon*, and *Trolls*.
- *Carnival* – Characters from Dr. Seuss stories such as the cat from *Cat in the Hat*, along with Thing 1 and Thing 2.
- *MSC Cruises* – Legos. Smurfs.

- *Norwegian* used to have a partnership with Nickelodeon, and they had character opportunities with Dora, SpongeBob, etc. That partnership ended in 2015. The line announced in October 2016 that the U.K.-based sports charity The Kings Foundation will provide kids programming across the entire fleet. The program will be a mix of entertainment and education, with an emphasis on family participation.

Please refer to Chapter 8 for a more detailed description of the kids' options offered on each of the major lines.

(2) Size of ship - The Rise of the Megaship

In recent years, the major cruise lines have been rolling out larger jumbo size cruise ships that can hold 4,000-5,000+ passengers plus a crew of 1500-2000 or more. The biggest of the big right now is *Royal Caribbean's Harmony of the Seas*, followed closely by its sister ships – *Oasis* and *Allure*. Megaships from other lines include *Norwegian's Epic, Escape, Breakaway* and *Getaway*; *Carnival's Vista* and *Breeze*; *Disney's Dream* and *Fantasy*.

The newer ships have been designed and built with dedicated facilities and activities for children. They also have a wider variety of stateroom configurations designed to accommodate families. The megaships tend to be the most family-friendly ships with the most varied and interesting programming that appeals to a wide range of children. Offerings may include elaborate water parks, rock climbing, child-friendly climbing walls, zip lines, bumper cars, ice and roller-skating, surf simulators, 3D movie theaters, and much more.

By contrast, some of the major cruise lines also have ships that serve 1,000 or less. These smaller ships are able to visit places the big ships cannot, but they do not generally offer special activities for small children.

(3) Dominant Players

This is a thumbnail sketch of each of the major cruise lines in the U.S. market (listed in alphabetical order). This is a high-level rough guide to assist you in preliminarily narrowing your options.

(a) Carnival

Carnival has a well-deserved reputation as the party cruise line. It features larger than average rooms and offers many short duration cruise options. It is very budget friendly and attracts younger independent travelers (as in groups of young people choosing to go on vacation vs. being carted along with their parents). It offers an extensive array of kids' programs, and many ships boast exceptional water play facilities.

(b) Celebrity

This is the upscale sister-line to *Royal Caribbean*. It has extensive spa offerings and numerous specialty gourmet restaurants. Innovative features include the hot glass show and the *Lawn Club* featuring real grass. It is comparable to *Princess* in price point. It has large, but not mega large ships. The dining room tends to be more formal.

(c) Disney
Disney ships are filled with families and children of all ages. Although this line fields only a small number of ships (4), it offers numerous amenities and bells/whistles, and some of the latest technology. *Disney* offers high-quality stage shows, fun pools with water slides, but no casinos. Stateroom configurations are notably family-friendly with 1 ½ split bathrooms and extra berth options. Prices tend to be substantially higher than the competition.

(d) Holland America
Holland America, which is now owned by *Carnival*, has a reputation for appealing to older cruisers—think grandparents and retirees. It is very traditional with offerings such as afternoon tea and ballroom dancing. Notwithstanding that reputation, it does have an established kids' program, but not as many kids as some of the players that are known to be family friendly. It has many enrichment classes in cooking and technology. It also has a reputation for offering better food. Many staterooms feature in-room DVD players and bathtubs. It also offers special promotions for family reunions and multigenerational cruising. Like *Princess*, it has an extensive presence in Alaska.

(e) MSC

MSC is a European-based line (Italy). It has been making aggressive efforts to establish itself in the North American market. *MSC Divina* is now based out of Miami and sails 7-day Caribbean sailings. Although *MSC* has reportedly made some efforts to appeal to the expectations of North American travelers, it still has a European ambiance. *MSC* offers some aggressive kids sail free promotions. *MSC* also offers its Yacht club, which is a premium luxury experience.

(f) Norwegian (NCL)

Norwegian has a reputation for being very informal and relaxed. The line features its signature "Freestyle" dining where cruisers set their own meal schedules. It is budget friendly, but its ships have smaller than typical staterooms. The line now offers a premium luxury experience in the "Haven" section of its ships. Several ships offer extensive water parks. It is the only cruise line to offer 7-day Hawaii cruises that start and end in Hawaii, as opposed to longer itineraries that start in California.

(g) Princess

Princess was once the featured ship on the television series *The Love Boat*. It is now owned by *Carnival*. *Princess* has a substantial kids' program, but overall the ships passengers tend to skew older. This line, generally, is not budget friendly and is more traditional in atmosphere, offerings, and dining. The line features a higher quality buffet than some of its competitors. And it stands out as one of the largest players in the Alaska market.

(h) Royal Caribbean

Royal Caribbean has some of the biggest and newest ships with all the bells and whistles, including *Harmony of the Seas* (currently the largest ship sailing), the other *Oasis* class ships, and the *Quantum class ships*. It boasts the largest cruise ships on the ocean – by a large margin. *Royal Caribbean* appeals to active travelers with many active onboard options like zip lines, surfing, rock climbing, etc. The breadth of activities and itineraries appeals to multigenerational families. It has some of the largest dedicated kids' club facilities of any line, and offers a wide range of entertainment options that include water-based shows and Broadway musicals. *Harmony* has a waterpark and a very large multi-story dry slide. A water slide is being added to *Adventure of the Seas* in late 2016. This line offers many budget-friendly options.

(4) Notable Omissions

There are numerous other cruise lines besides the eight that I have highlighted above, but for various reasons, they are not top candidates for consideration for most families traveling with small children (at least those families who are based in North America). Who has been excluded? There are several lines that are viewed as more "luxury" lines. These are the ones that do not necessarily cater to families with kids—*Crystal Cruises*,

Silversea, Regent Seven Seas. There are also cruise lines that focus on offering river cruises. Generally, river cruises involve smaller ships and are geared more toward older travelers. At times, however, there may be themed cruises that attract families and/or may otherwise appeal to children.

If you would like a summary overview of the youth policies and programs for these additional cruise lines, you may download a free copy of the *Family Cruise Companion's Reference Guide on Cruise Line Youth Programs.* Please visit *http://familycruisecompanion.com/free-youth-summary* to obtain your copy. This booklet provides key highlights for more than 50 different cruise lines, and it can be used as a quick reference guide when doing your own cruise research and planning.

D. Selecting a cabin

The type of cabin you choose could have the biggest impact on your budget. A family traveling in an inside cabin will likely pay thousands of dollars less than one traveling on the same ship, same itinerary in a balcony room or suite. This large spread in price points is one reason why groups of families can plan trips together and accommodate a wide range of price points.

(i) Factors to consider

The primary consideration in evaluating cabins will most likely be what you can afford. But other key distinguishing features between staterooms include: whether you want access to natural light (interior rooms have no windows); whether you require direct access to fresh air (requires at least a balcony); and the size of your travel party.

A significant factor to consider is how much time you think you and your family members will actually spend in the room. If you believe that your cabin will primarily be a place to sleep, bathe, and store your luggage, then the actual size of the cabin and various amenities are likely less important to you. Interior rooms or oceanview rooms could be quite comfortable and affordable. If, however, you know that members of your party love to lounge around in quarters from time to time, or you have four or more people, then you should pay close attention to the actual square footage of your cabin.

When you are making a reservation, you will have the opportunity to select a specific cabin. If you have concerns about motion sickness, the location of your cabin may assist in addressing that. Generally, you will want cabins that have less of a tendency to magnify the motion of the ship. This means you would want one of the lower levels and a room closer to mid-ship. Cabins that are on the highest levels and closer to one of the ends of the ship will feel more of the ship's motion on the water.

Likewise, if you are sensitive to noise—or otherwise have noise concerns, you should avoid the decks that are directly below the pool deck, and rooms that are in close proximity to bars, lounges, and other high traffic areas. Also, cabins that are located on the lower decks and toward one of the extreme ends of the ship are more likely to hear the ship's mechanical noises.

(2) Types of accommodations

The typical fare structure for a standard cabin has a full fare price for the first two passengers and a heavily discounted price for passengers three and four. Please note that, although some cabins are designed to hold 4 passengers, depending on the capacity of the ship they are not able to actually book 4 passengers in all of those cabins.

Standard staterooms come in various sleeping configurations. Some cabins may have a sofa bed with a twin size bed that pulls down from the ceiling. Or, a cabin may have a sofa bed that sleeps two and two single beds that can be pushed together or be kept separate. The information specific to individual cabins can usually be found online on the cruise line's website in the section regarding deck plans for individual ships. Generally, there are no roll-aways. There are some pack n' plays available, which are used as cribs. Those should be requested in advance.

(a) Inside staterooms

Inside staterooms are rooms without windows. They are usually the smallest sized cabin and will have the cheapest rate. These rooms could be ideal for people who will not spend much time in their cabin and/or who are indifferent to the lack of natural light. These rooms can also be great options if you are booking multiple cabins, and book it as part of a broader mix of cabins that will be more or less shared as family space. So, for instance, we have traveled with a large family group where some had a family balcony, and some had an inside stateroom, and everyone hung out on the very large balcony in the family stateroom.

(b) Oceanview

An oceanview room will be similar in size to an inside cabin, but will have a window or a porthole. This provides the benefit of natural light and somewhat of a view. But the actual size of window varies based on the ship. It could be a small, obstructed porthole. You can find out specific information about the size of window and possible obstructions for any individual cabin directly from the cruise line – some information is available on the website – and you or your travel agent can get more information by calling.

Please note that Disney has introduced the concept of a "virtual" porthole; apparently, these rooms have become quite popular. They basically consist of an inside room with a special video monitor that reflects the view of what is happening outside the ship. Sometimes *Disney* characters will pop up in the feed as well.

(c) Balcony

A traditional balcony cabin will be similar to an oceanview cabin, but it will have an attached private deck that you can physically access from the stateroom. The balcony will typically have at least a table and a couple of chairs. It may also include loungers and other furniture. Some ships now offer other types of "balcony" rooms that don't involve the ocean. *Royal Caribbean* on its *Oasis* class ships offers balconies that face the internal Central Park. It also offers "virtual" balconies on its newest ship, *Harmony*.

Advantages of a balcony room include access to fresh air and extra space to roam, which can be good during nap times or when you want a bit of quiet. They can be a great option for people who like to read or lounge in the sun without the distractions of the pool environs. A balcony can be particularly advantageous for certain itineraries, such as Alaska, where some days are largely "scenic cruising." When booking, you should specifically inquire as to the availability of any "family" balcony rooms (you should specifically use the word "family"). These rooms are often larger than the standard balcony rooms and will rival a suite in size, but not in price. Not surprisingly, the "family" rooms tend to sell out quickly. [Note: In 2017, *Royal Caribbean* announced plans to change the names for all of its stateroom categories starting in 2018. "Family" cabins will be re-named "Spacious" or "Ultra spacious."]

Many parents are understandably concerned about small children having access to balconies. It can be very nerve-wracking to see your small child leaning against Plexiglas, and realize that a sheet of plastic is all that is separating him from a 40+ foot fall. Industry standards require that the balcony walls be at least 42 inches. Which is great as most toddlers do not reach this height. But the reality is that there are several pieces of deck furniture that can be climbed upon rendering walls much shorter and toddlers much taller. Bottom line – lots of safety precautions have been taken, but small children must still be supervised at *all* times while outside on the balcony.

(d) Suites

Suites are typically larger cabins that, at a minimum, will have a defined living space that is separate from the sleeping area. There will typically be a comfortable balcony. Most ships will have several different types of suites with increasing levels of size and price. In addition to more space, suites will also come with many premium amenities. These may include high-end toiletries, high-quality robes and slippers, early access to reservations, and VIP treatment at embarkation and disembarkation. They will also often include increased cabin service such as a butler or more focused and frequent attention from a room attendant. Suite passengers may also have access to certain designated exclusive venues such as certain specialty restaurants, lounges, spa facilities or pools. These accommodations come with a significantly larger price tag. Suites often start out at double the cost of a balcony room per person. Suites will typically have large balconies, and some may have 180-degree wrap-around balconies.

(e) Other considerations

If your family needs more space, but a suite is not a viable option financially, there are other options to consider. Some ships offer cabins with connecting doors, while some also have connecting balconies. Some lines have "family" cabins that are charged out at a reasonable rate, but they fill up very quickly. You could also consider booking one balcony or oceanview room and the adjacent inside room. Family members who are sleeping in the interior room could share the balcony.

So that you can have a better sense as to how room types compare across different cruise lines, ships and categories, here are some real world examples. This snapshot comparison is based on research conducted on the relevant cruise line websites. Specifically, this is published pricing for *Caribbean* cruises sailing in late July 2017—specifically, embarkation dates of July 29 or July 30. As of the date of the research, the prospective cruises were about 8 to 9 months out. All prices presented below are per person, based on double occupancy, and do not include taxes or port fees. Information regarding suites is for the entry level in that category.

- *Carnival Vista* – July 29 8-Day Southern Caribbean (Miami) (*newer ship*)
  - Interior ($1174): 185 s.f.
  - Oceanview ($1459): 185 s.f./220 s.f.
  - Balcony ($1754): 185 s.f. with balcony of 35 s.f. (some have 60-75)
  - Suite (N/A): 275 s.f. with balcony of 65 s.f.
  Note: Suites were sold out for this sailing. However, the June 17 sailing had comparable pricing structure and Suites started at $2979.

- **Carnival Magic** – July 29 7-Day Eastern Caribbean (Orlando)
  - Interior ($984): 185 s.f.
  - Oceanview ($1084): 185 s.f./220 s.f.
  - Balcony ($1284): 185 s.f. with balcony of 35-75 s.f.
  - Suite ($2449): 275 s.f. with balcony of 35 s.f. or 65 s.f.
- **Royal Caribbean Harmony of the Seas** – July 29 7-Night Western Caribbean (Fort Lauderdale) (*newer ship*)
  - Interior ($1299): 149-172 s.f.
  - Oceanview ($1499): 179-199 s.f.
  - Balcony ($1548): 182 s.f. with balcony of 50-80 s.f.
  - Suite ($3407): 287 s.f. with balcony of 80 s.f. (Junior Suite)
- **Royal Caribbean Allure of the Seas** – July 30 7-night Eastern Caribbean (Fort Lauderdale)
  - Interior ($1086): 149-172 s.f.
  - Oceanview($1280): 179 s.f.
  - Balcony ($1299): 182 s.f. with balcony of 50-82 s.f.
  - Suite ($2199): 287 s.f. with balcony of 80 s.f. (Junior Suite)
- **Norwegian Escape** – July 29 7-Day Eastern Caribbean (Miami)
  - Interior ($899): 135-201 s.f.
  - Oceanview ($1099): 161-252 s.f.
  - Balcony ($1249): 207-239 s.f. (includes balcony of 43 s.f.)
  - Suite ($1399): 239-513 s.f. (includes balcony of 43 s.f.) (mini-suite)

- **Celebrity Equinox** – July 30 7-Day Western Caribbean (Miami)
  - Interior ($999): 177 s.f.
  - Oceanview ($1286): 177 s.f.
  - Balcony ($1586): 194 s.f. with 54 s.f. balcony
  - Suite ($2723:) 300 s.f. with 74 s.f. balcony
- **Disney Fantasy** – July 29 7-Night Eastern Caribbean (Port Canaveral)
  - Interior ($2464): 169 s.f.
  - Oceanview ($2520): 202 s.f.
  - Balcony ($2674): 246 s.f.
  - Concierge ($5159): 306 s.f.

  Note: Disney quotes fares based on cabin. The per person price listed above was calculated based on quote for 2 person cabin less taxes and port fees.
- **Princess** – NO JULY 2017 CARIBBEAN SAILINGS
- **Holland America** –NO JULY 2017 CARIBBEAN SAILINGS

E. Travel Insurance

Most cruises are fully refundable until the final payment date—typically 90 days in advance of embarkation date. After the final payment date, any cancellations will come with a monetary penalty that increases the closer you get to embarkation date – anywhere from 25% to 100%. Given the relative expense, and the wide range of life events that can pop up or things that can go wrong in the three months before a cruise, purchasing some type of travel insurance is prudent.

Every cruise line will offer its own version of travel insurance. Various travel agents will have other options. Note that not all policies are created equal and you do not necessarily have to purchase directly from the cruise line. In many instances, the cruise line offering may not be your best option.

Common features of a comprehensive policy include coverage for trip interruption, trip cancellation, trip delay or missed connections, baggage loss or delay, medical expenses, medical evacuation, repatriation, involuntary job loss, or pregnancy. A good policy will extend coverage when these events happen to you, or you have to cancel because the event happens to a travel companion. You will also want a policy that provides full reimbursement regardless of when a cancellation occurs.

One potential negative factor to look for when examining policies offered through the cruise line (or elsewhere) is whether it is secondary coverage, rather than primary coverage – meaning that the secondary policy will only apply once you have attempted to obtain payment from your other insurance sources, such as homeowners, private medical, credit cards, etc. You should also check whether reimbursement comes in the form of credit for a future cruise as opposed to cash, or under what circumstances only credit is available. Also, you should be aware that a cruise line policy usually will not apply to instances where the cruise line itself experiences a financial default – i.e., your cruise is canceled because the cruise line went out of business.

You do not have to purchase the insurance at the time of your initial booking, but you should plan to pay for it at or before the deadline for final payment. (I typically purchase it at the same time that I make my final payment.)

You should be mindful of the review period for the policy. You will have some period of time to review the policy closely and change your mind for a full refund of the policy premium – usually about 10 days. Thereafter, the premium is non-refundable. If you purchase the policy too early, you could face the situation where you cancel or change your cruise prior to the final payment deadline without penalty, but cannot get a refund on the insurance – a policy that is no longer of any use to you.

For your reference, a list of some of the major providers of travel insurance can be found in the appendix of this book, as well as a list of some insurance comparison sites. See Appendix.

CHAPTER 3

REGISTRATION & PRE-EMBARKATION PLANNING

At some point prior to your embarkation day, you will be provided the opportunity to register online. Registration basically involves providing relevant identifying information required to travel for every member of your party – *e.g.*, citizenship information, emergency contacts. During this pre-embarkation period, you will also have the opportunity to purchase numerous products, services, and packages for your upcoming trip such as beverage packages, internet packages, spa services, shore excursions, and other reservations for entertainment, recreation or specialty dining. Some of these packages may be offered at a discounted price from what will be offered on-board.

A. Beverages
You will be offered a variety of beverage packages that cover different combinations of alcoholic and/or non-alcoholic drinks. Available packages vary across different lines and categories of drinks. You should be aware that not all alcoholic

drinks receive the same treatment, nor do all non-alcoholic beverages. The alcohol packages may draw distinctions based on beer and wine vs. hard liquor and cocktails, and/or place a cap on the dollar value of an individual drink that may be covered by the package. Similarly, packages for non-alcoholic beverages may draw distinctions based on type of beverage; *e.g.*, bottled water (and/or brand of water), specialty coffees, juices and soda, energy drinks, or mock-tails. So, if you have a preference for premium liquor and cocktails vs. beer and wine, or specialty coffees (*e.g.*, lattes) and bottled water, you need to make sure that your favorites are covered.

Typically, the packages are quoted as a "daily" charge, but you pay a flat fee based on the total number of days of the cruise, regardless of how many sea days or port days are available. (So, for instance, a package on a 7-day cruise that is touted at $40/day unlimited beverages – will cost $280 for one person.) Generally, packages that include various alcohol combinations will range from $55.00 to $79 per day, and non-alcoholic packages will range from $18 to $25. You should also note that the package will also come with a surcharge for gratuities of 15-18%. Packages are sold on an individual basis; meaning that it will be linked to a specific passenger account and you will not be permitted to share.

As you are evaluating whether a drink package is right for you and your family members—and if so, which ones—you should keep in mind that virtually all beverages beyond generic coffee, tea, and water (and on some ships, juice at breakfast time) will incur a charge. So the best way to evaluate whether a package is right for you is to estimate how many drinks per day you will typically drink (both alcoholic and non-alcoholic) and do the math. Assume the prices for individual drinks will be similar to what you would pay at a hotel resort. So, for instance, I would use $3 to $6 for non-alcoholic drinks and $8-12 for alcohol. Keep in mind that the same daily rate applies whether it is a sea day or a port day.

As a rule of thumb, you should try to figure out whether you are likely to drink 5 or more beverages a day after breakfast. Most of your typical breakfast beverages will be complimentary at breakfast – coffee, tea, milk, juice, etc. So, if after breakfast, you are likely only to have a beverage at lunch, another one or two at dinner, and perhaps one more at some other point during the day, you would probably be better served paying *a la carte*. Conversely, if you know that in addition to beer at lunch and wine at dinner, you will likely consume several specialty coffees over the course of the day, have a cocktail or two by the pool, and indulge in a couple of drinks after hours in the casino, you will probably get full value out of a beverage package.

I have almost always ended up having one – either purchasing it outright or selecting it as an optional perk under some applicable promotion. But, many times when I purchased a package outright, I have felt like I did not really get full value. This is particularly true for some cruises where I purchased packages for one of my children.

You should also be aware that the cruise lines will have restrictions on what beverages can be brought on board. These limitations typically relate to alcohol, but apparently, some cruises have started restricting even bottled water. If you attempt to bring aboard more alcohol than permitted – either at the beginning of the cruise or during port days – these items will be confiscated and stored and returned to you at disembarkation. Notwithstanding these limitations, some passengers attempt to smuggle additional alcohol on board in various concealed containers. Many of these types of items can be found on Google or through Amazon. (I make this point solely to inform you of your options, not to advocate skirting the rules.)

If you are interested in a beverage package, you should definitely check whether the line is offering any discounts for purchasing the packages in advance online. Such discounts can be substantial – *e.g.*, 30% – for some of the more expensive premium packages.

B. Shore Excursions

When you pre-register for your cruise online, you will also have the opportunity to reserve shore excursions for the different ports that your ship will visit. Typically, the cruise line will present a wide range of offerings that appeal to a wide range of people and encompass various types of activities. There may be city tours, beach tours, adventure activities like zip lining, helicopters, cooking lessons, and/or other activities that are representative of the locale being visited. The descriptions for these excursions will usually provide information as to level of physical activity required (minimal to strenuous), amount of walking or interim travel time, any age restrictions, and other pertinent information. To the extent that the excursions have not filled up, you will also have the opportunity to book while onboard. Usually, when you book in advance, you also pay in advance. When you book on board, the charges are applied to your shipboard account.

C. Photographs

Depending on the cruise line and the sailing, you may also have the opportunity to purchase a photo package in advance. Throughout your cruise, you will have many opportunities to have photos snapped by professional photographers. This starts with a photography station set up near the embarkation area where you can get a photo of your party as it is about to set off on its adventure. Every morning when you reach a new port, there will be several photographers waiting to greet you as you step off the ship. If you are on a ship with characters, there will be numerous photo stations set up throughout your voyage. There will be photo stations set outside the main dining rooms and other central venues, and there will be roaming photographers taking pictures at your table in the dining room. You have no obligation to purchase any of these photos.

You will have the opportunity to go to the photo shop on board throughout your cruise, review the photos, and decide whether to purchase any or all of them. On some ships, you also have the option to review the photos on the television in your stateroom.

Purchasing copies of these professional photos can be quite pricey– either as prints or as digital files. Typically, a single print can range from $10-$20 or more. These overall costs can be reduced through purchasing photo packages. These are packages that allow you to purchase either a certain number of prints/files or copies of all of the prints or files or both.

Oftentimes there will be an opportunity to purchase discounted packages prior to sailing. So, for example, you will often find a package that includes all prints and all digital files for around $300-$400. There may also be print only or digital only versions of the package for less. If you opt to purchase a package, you should try to maximize the value. Since all photos are included, have everyone take photos at every opportunity. An all-inclusive package covers every photo that includes a passenger registered to your cabin– so take them at every opportunity. If traveling with friends or family in another cabin, take photos together and share costs. Although you may be offered discounted photo packages that are said to only be available prior to embarkation, I have also found that additional discounted packages may be available for purchase during the first 2-3 days of the cruise.

A word of caution: If you have pre-purchased a package, check in with the photography staff relatively early in your trip to make sure that they have a proper record of your purchase. Make sure that they are correctly gathering all of the photos that are affiliated with your cabin. (This is done through facial recognition software.) Regardless of whether you pre-purchase a package, you should avoid waiting until the last minute to review photographs. If you wait until the last sailing day, you may encounter large crowds and cranky confusion. Also, in some circumstances, you have the potential to get shut out. You typically cannot order prints the day of disembarkation or after you leave, and all unpurchased photos are usually destroyed at the conclusion of each sailing.

D. Other Reservations

You may have an opportunity to make advanced reservations for items such as specialty restaurants, headliner shows, and spa services. The key advantage to booking these types of items in advance is the opportunity to lock in your preferred schedule. Sometimes there may also be discounts associated with pre-booking as well. If you are unable to make reservations in advance, you should make a point of doing so during your first day on the cruise.

In my experience, there are two situations where you are actively competing with other passengers to get to do what you want – activities on sea days and activities on days that the ship docks at a private island. In both situations, the options are defined and while numerous – they are not infinite. If you have the opportunity to pre-book activities that you will enjoy on sea days, you should take advantage of it.

CHAPTER 4

PLANNING FOR ON-SHORE ACTIVITIES

Since you have booked a cruise that travels between several different ports, you are probably interested in getting off the ship to see them. There are several different ways to do that: you can book excursions through the cruise line (either online before you leave, or onboard at the shore excursions desk); you can book through independent tour operators; or you can wing it, and step off the ship and just see what happens.

A. Booking through cruise line

Whether you book in advance online, or book once you are on-board the ship, the cruise line will present a wide range of shore excursions. These are activities and local tour operators that have been vetted by the cruise line. All payments for these activities will be made through the cruise line. Most of these activities will be set up to accommodate a large group of people.

Booking through the cruise line is usually the easiest and most convenient way to fill out your itinerary. However, it is also most likely one of the most expensive ways.

A key advantage of booking a shore excursion through the cruise line is that you don't have to worry about getting back to the ship on time. (I am sure you have seen those videos of screaming passengers making a mad dash down the pier as the ship pulls away. If not, do a search on *YouTube*.) The ship is guaranteed to wait for you if there are delays returning to port. Similarly, any changes in the ship's itinerary will be accommodated automatically. Also, these tours offer the most flexibility as to switching and reasons for switching. You can still change your mind while on board up until a couple of days before. If someone in your party is sick, you can often get a refund. If the tour is canceled for some reason (e.g., ship pulls into port too late; unexpected logistical problems with tour operator), you will be issued a prompt refund.

Not surprisingly, convenience and reliability come with a premium price. Excursions booked through the cruise line will be more expensive than comparable tours that you could arrange on your own if you had the time and knowledge to do so. Some of the most attractive excursions may sell out quickly. You also have to contend with moving around in a large group (think motor coach or bus vs. small van or taxi).

When you are assessing your options for shore excursions, you should look for and read any fine print and determine whether there are age (or other) restrictions for participating. Assuming your children are within any existing age restrictions, they will usually be charged a reduced rate. In some cases, small children (under 3) will not be charged at all. (If your children fall outside the permissible age range, you may have the option to leave them on board. See Chapter 8 for summary of policies for different cruise lines.)

There will be some type of brochure that provides a detailed description of the excursion, including the mode of transportation, the level of physical activity, and the total length of the excursion, including any required travel time. You should pay attention to any information provided about travel times and assess whether your family is up to it. For instance, is it a 5-hour excursion that involves an hour of travel each way? What is the mode of travel – a long bus ride where you are seated the entire time? A catamaran or small boat where refreshments are offered, and you can walk around? Will there be long walks over uneven ground that is not conducive to a stroller, or small, tired feet? If for some reason your crew poops out midway through the excursion, you may not be able to terminate your participation early (as least not easily), so you should consider the overall stamina of your group in advance.

B. Independent Arrangements

Although booking through the cruise line may be the path of least resistance, it is not your only option. If you booked your cruise through a large travel agency, they will often have arrangements with other tour operators and will offer their own slate of options available in different ports. These are often cheaper than what is being offered by the cruise line and often involve smaller groups. Likewise, you can do your own research and book with local tour operators directly.

So, for instance, if the primary activity for a given day is to go to the beach, you should take a hard look at options beyond what is being offered by the cruise line. There are lots of comparable options – and perhaps the same option – available at lower prices.

An advantage to booking outside the cruise line is that you can often find better value and more flexibility as to content. A key disadvantage is that your advance plans do not as easily adapt to changes in the ship's schedule. If there is a last minute itinerary change, the burden of making any adjustments falls entirely on you. Moreover, if for some reason your independent tour runs late, you potentially have a major problem. If the ship leaves without you, you are responsible for making your way to the next port to catch up with it.

Also, you may have some difficulty in assessing quality in advance. You must make sure that your chosen operator or vendor is reliable. You can do this by checking review sites such as *TripAdvisor*. You can also connect with people via "roll calls" on *Cruise Critic* or *Facebook*.

In addition to potentially being cheaper, your independent arrangements may also involve smaller groups with more comfortable modes of transportation. And, you control more of the schedule.

One of the best shore excursions I ever had was arranged independently through a company I found online.

The content and schedule were perfectly tailored to the disparate members of our group. They were able to design a tour that visited every site our group was interested in seeing. Our English-speaking driver ferried us around in a very comfortable minivan. At times, we were able to split up and meet back with our driver at a designated time and spot. And we were able to take a leisurely lunch break on our schedule. It was perfectly executed at a great price. It made going back to regular cruise line excursions somewhat difficult.

If you disembark the ship for your own independent excursion, you should be mindful of the time the ship is in port. As you depart, there will be an "all aboard" time posted (one for crew and one for passengers). You should make sure you know it. You should also make sure that you stay on "ship time." The ship may not make adjustments as it crosses time zones, so you should not rely on your electronic devices because these will often reset to local time. You should plan to be back at least ½ hour before the time everyone is instructed to return. This will give you somewhat of a buffer against unexpected traffic delays; and it may also help avoid long lines to get back on the ship.

C. Winging it

For those who are truly adventurous at heart, or who are not that interested in detailed pre-planning, there is also the option to simply wing it. Basically, you plan to exit the ship and see what options await you at the port. Oftentimes there will be some sort of tourist information desk or collection of tour operators close to the pier. You can wander over and check out those options. You also could simply hop in a taxi or nearby public transportation and go exploring. Usually, in the newsletter provided the evening before in your stateroom, there will be some general information about the port, the layout of the pier, some type of map of the vicinity, and emergency contact information. There may also be some information about what you should expect to pay for taxi or bus rides. Take this with you as you set out to explore.

There will usually be some shops/stands that you will encounter shortly after disembarking. These will have a variety of souvenirs and tourist items. Keep in mind that these vendors will likely have more expensive items than you will find if you venture farther into town. Also, if you elect to sign up with a tour operator or excursion on shore, you should be mindful that these operators will not necessarily have been vetted by anyone, so proceed with caution.

In general, the "wing it" option can be a risky proposition. You are in a strange place, you will obviously be a tourist (if for no other reason than you just stepped off a large cruise ship), and you can easily be placed at a disadvantage. This can be mitigated if you are with a group of people – either your original travel group or folks you connect with on board.

I have used the pure winging it approach a handful of times with mixed results. (I have never done the "winging it" option with small children in tow, however.) Once, we ended up with a driver who kept nodding off as we were driving around some hairpin curves in the mountains. Quite nerve-wracking. A couple of times, we have just walked off the ship to walk around and see what can be seen. Note – usually there is not a lot of stuff to be seen that is walking distance from the port. Lots of higher priced tourist souvenirs; or alternatively, some townsfolk selling handmade goods. Some port research will let you know which ports do or do not have easily accessible activities near the port. Not surprisingly, bigger cities and/or smaller islands tend to have some viable options.

D. Remaining on Board
Finally, you should remember that you are not required to get off at every port. You can create a fun or relaxing day for yourself on the ship. This is a great time to leisurely explore the ship. If you choose to stay on board, you can enjoy the pool, spa, specialty attractions, etc., and have much less competition for the popular spots. You will likely encounter large discounts on spa services on port days. Note, however, that revenue based venues will typically be closed while in port – e.g., the shops, the casino.

CHAPTER 5

PACKING FOR YOUR TRIP

You have likely been on some type of family vacation before, and you have some general sense of how you like to pack for your family. Assuming that you have a basic foundation, I simply want to highlight a few things that you should keep in mind as you are specifically packing for a cruise. (For your convenience, you can also download a copy of a *Family Cruise Prep & Pack Checklist* to assist you. Please visit *http://familycruisecompanion.com/prep-and-pack-list* to get your copy.)

A. General Packing Tips

First, space is at a premium—particularly storage space. As a general rule of thumb, a standard stateroom will have sufficient drawer and closet space to accommodate the belongings of two adults. As you can see from the stateroom information provided in Chapter 2, typical non-suite cabins run about 165 to 195 square feet. (Contrast this with typical U.S. hotel rooms that run about 300 to 400 square feet.) While you should be mindful of over-packing and bringing too much stuff on board generally, you should also be mindful of how many pieces of luggage you bring and whether they can be easily stored in your stateroom. Ideally, you will be able to "nest" some pieces of luggage inside others—for instance, either because some pieces are smaller in overall size than others or because you have soft/flexible luggage that can be stuffed into larger pieces. It would be ideal if your luggage could fit under the bed so that it is not in the way or otherwise taking up valuable closet space.

Second, also because space is at a premium, you will ideally want to pack in such a fashion that your clothes and personal items are organized for easy retrieval. This can be done using packing cubes, large Ziploc bags, or a combination of both methods.

I find it helpful to make some type of list based on categories of items and needs of individual family members. This is a good time to figure out whether you will be dressing up for any formal nights, whether/how often you will want to change for dinner (after a day of excursions or beach activities) and what gear you may need that will likely not be provided on or available on the ship. For example, your stateroom will likely have its own hair dryer so you can leave yours at home. You will also have easy access to beach towels that you can use on and off the ship. Some cruise lines will also make swimming vests available for children to use at the pool, but not to take off the ship.

You should also bring something to help manage your family's electronics. If your family has multiple electronic devices that require periodic charging, you should also pack something to expand the number of outlets available. Typically, there will not be very many electrical outlets in your cabin. So you will want a device that can transform one outlet into 4, 6 or more. Different cruise lines have different rules or practices as to whether power strips are permitted and how large they can be. And these are often not consistently enforced. These days it is possible to find small palm-sized outlet expanders that have slots for multiple USB charge cords. If many or most of your devices can be charged using a USB port, then this would be a great option.

As a final tip, remember that a tablet can be your best friend when traveling – both on and off the ship. Consider picking up a cheap one (*e.g.*, Amazon often has Fire tablets for under $50). And, ideally, everyone can have his or her own device. Tablets can be great for downtime in your room, providing entertainment on a long bus ride (with headphones), or during other long waiting periods. A tablet's also good if you don't like the limited options available on the cruise ship television.

B. Packing for Infants/Toddlers/Small Children

If your travel party includes infants or toddlers, you must be more detail oriented in planning your packing. Pack carefully. Do not assume that you will have easy access to purchase necessary items that you forget or use up. Make a list identifying things that you would be very sad not to have for 3 days, *e.g.*, items such as diapers, wipes, formula, preferred pain medication, and sanitary products. Many items are not carried on board or can easily run out. Also, you will not always be able to find what you want when you want at any given port. So, for example, rather than your typical pain reliever, you may only be able to find unbranded kids' pain medication where everything is written in Spanish (or other language) that you do not understand. Although you can often find usual sundries on board – they may quickly run out of your preferred item. (Once I was on a ship that inexplicably had run out of ibuprofen of any kind by the second day, and we had two back-to-back sea days.)

For young children, you should consider bringing an umbrella stroller. It will be useful when trying to move quickly about the ship and at the airport, etc. But be mindful that for some shore excursions it can be more of a burden – if there are numerous steps, uneven ground, or all sand. That said, while a stroller can be a real pain at the beach, I always persevered when my kids were babies/toddlers because it was a great secure way for kids to nap (under umbrella).

I would strongly discourage you from taking any large deluxe Cadillac type stroller that you might have. A truly bulky stroller will take up way too much space in your room, even when folded up. Also, some larger strollers may not fit easily through the door of your cabin when the stroller is in the open position. Seriously. I was traveling with a friend who encountered this problem, and she basically had to carry her baby out into the hallway in order to place him in the open stroller. It made it very inconvenient to get in and out of stateroom easily.

You should pack materials to wash out your baby bottles, sippy cups, and dishes – this includes a small bottle of dish soap and brush. Do not expect to find suitable dish soap. Something else to consider is a small electric bottle sterilizer. *Disney* has some available for passengers through guest services. Otherwise, you can pack your own.

C. A Word About Laundry

To facilitate streamlining your packing, you can bring some single use laundry detergent to wash some small items in the sink and hang dry. There should be some type of clothesline in the bathroom. For larger items, there will certainly be a laundry option on board, but it may be expensive. Some, but not all, cruise lines also offer self-serve laundry rooms that are relatively inexpensive, and in some instances, may be complementary. Truly complementary self-serve laundry facilities are found on the smaller luxury vessels.

The following cruise lines do not offer any self-serve laundry facilities: *Celebrity, Costa, MSC, Norwegian, Royal Caribbean*, and *Windstar*. *Holland America* offers pay based self-serve laundry facilities on some, but not all ships. The following lines offer self-serve laundry facilities that are coin operated or for which guests otherwise pay: *Carnival, Disney, Holland America, Princess*, and *Silversea*. The following lines offer complementary self-serve laundry: *Azamara Club, Crystal, Cunard, Oceania, Regent Seven Seas*, and *Seabourn*.

Please note that you will not be permitted to have an iron or steamer in your cabin. These items will be confiscated if found. The ship will offer pressing service for a fee. Another alternative is to pack some type of wrinkle away spray.

You can download a convenient checklist that incorporates the key information discussed above-the *Family Cruise Prep & Pack Checklist*. Please visit *http://familycruisecompanion. com/prep-and-pack-list* to download your copy.

CHAPTER 6

EMBARKATION DAY

A. Traveling from Your Home to the Ship

As you are making plans to transport your family to the port city that will be the starting point for your cruise, you will have to decide when you will arrive – the same day as your scheduled embarkation or in advance?

The safest, more conservative course of action is to arrive the day before. This provides an ample buffer for potential mishaps such as delayed/missed flights or wayward luggage. This option will incur an additional hotel expense and some additional logistical burdens associated with navigating you, your family, and its luggage from airport to hotel, and again from hotel to ship.

Although conventional wisdom advises arriving at least one day early, that is not our standard operating procedure. Unless I am going to a new city or am departing from a port in a foreign country, I much prefer to schedule my flights for the same day as the starting date for the cruise. Our flight to Florida is not that long (less than 3 hours), and there are multiple reliable options each day. Because I feel comfortable arriving on the same day, we avoid incurring an extra hotel expense, and we avoid the logistical burdens of having to schlepp our luggage from the airport to a hotel and back. For ports in foreign cities, I usually arrive at least one day early, so as to account for possible travel delays and flight cancellations. For cities that are destinations, which can be part of the kick-off to our vacation (e.g., Acapulco, Barcelona, Hong Kong), I plan on arriving a few days in advance. This also allows time to address any jet lag issues.

Regardless of whether you fly on the same day or the day before, I strongly advise you to make advance airport transport arrangements. You can find recommendations and reviews for such services through simple Internet searches. Even though this may be a little more expensive than a regular taxi, it is worth it. You can skip the long cab lines, guarantee that you have a vehicle sufficient to transport the right number of people and luggage, and start off your trip a little more comfortably.

Our first few cruises out of Florida, I went the traditional taxi route and (with the exception of one childless cruise) was miserable every time. The line was very long, and the wait was very hot and humid. Once we got to the front of the line, we were usually shunted off to the side to wait for a van or other larger vehicle that could accommodate the size of our party and all of its luggage and gear. Standing in the heat for close to an hour with a cranky, crying baby started the trip off on a sour note.

Another advantage to pre-booking airport transport is that you can minimize language issues and/or money disputes. With a pre-arranged ride, the driver already knows your exact destination and how to get there, and you already know the price you are supposed to be paying.

B. Boarding Your Ship
(1) The Luggage Process

Once you arrive at the pier, someone will be there to take charge of your luggage. If you pre-registered, you will have had the opportunity to arrange for pre-printed luggage tags. These are tags that have all the information that will allow the crewmembers to direct your bags to your specific cabin. If you do not have the pre-printed tags, the pier-side personnel will be able to write ones up for you by hand.

As you watch all of your bags being wheeled away on giant carts with hundreds of other bags, you should assume that you will not see your luggage again for several hours. For this reason, you should plan to keep any essential items or valuables with you. Also, this is the last time that you will see the person handling your luggage, so if you are inclined to provide a tip, you should do so now.

(2) Check-in and Boarding

Once you have tendered your luggage, you will enter the actual pier facility, and you will go through a security checkpoint – similar to what you see at the airport but more low-key. After security, you will go to the appropriate registration line and check in. There you will confirm whatever method of payment you want to use for onboard charges, the check-in agent will take photos of you and every member of your party (for security purposes), and you will receive your cruise card.

Your cruise card serves many important purposes. It is the key to your stateroom. You are required to swipe it at security every time you exit or board the ship (and your photo will pop up on a security screen so that security can confirm you are who you say you are). And, the card is used for any and all purchases made on-board. Typically, your cruise card is the sole currency used on-board. No cash or credit cards are used. Basically, you will be running a tab throughout your cruise, and you will settle up at the end. If you want to check on your account and/or make an interim payment, you can do so at Guest Services. Otherwise, the final balance will be charged to whatever credit card you have on file. (Depending on the cruise line and ship, you will also be able to check on your bill using the television in your stateroom.)

It may take several hours for your luggage to arrive. So you should consider packing a swimsuit and sun items in a day bag that stays with you. Also, the timing of your embarkation can make food options tricky. It could be that the dining areas are not open or are about to close (either due to regular hours or in anticipation of the mandatory muster). For those that are open, they could be jam-packed because of thousands of people boarding in a short space of time. Pack a snack to tide you over.

C. Settling into your stateroom
(i) Unpacking/setting up to maximize space and utility

Once your luggage arrives at your cabin, you should plan to unpack fully, and you should encourage all family members to do so as well. Everyone will be much more comfortable if you are not continually pulling suitcases out to look for things. If you packed using packing cubes to organize your stuff, you can pull them right out of the suitcase and drop them in the drawers. Once your bags are empty, you should nest luggage as best you can and place under the bed.

In most standard staterooms, storage space will be at a premium, particularly if you are trying to accommodate the belongings of more than two people. Your stateroom will have some combination of closets, drawers, and shelves. There will be hangers provided in the closet, and you should utilize them. Drawer space is often at premium, so you should plan to hang some clothes where practical. If you find that you need additional hangers, you can request them from your stateroom attendant. If you are on a newer ship, you should look for "hidden" storage spaces behind mirrors or wood paneling. Sometimes you may be pleasantly surprised to find additional shelves or cubbies. If you do not find any, you should ask your stateroom attendant whether you have overlooked anything.

Employing some simple organizational tools can help prevent your stateroom from feeling cramped. If you are interested in maximizing your available space and making it more comfortable for your family, there are several convenience items that you can bring along with you to help you make the most use of your available space. These are all items that are often recommended by veteran cruisers. First, I always take a set of foldable hanging shelves for the closet – like the ones you use for sweaters. These come in many variations, but the best one for this purpose are the kind that has some kind of a stiff or supported bottom to each shelf, and where the entire unit folds up easily into a single square for easy packing. A set of these will substantially multiply your available drawer space. And, you can use them to store just about anything – clothes, shoes, swim gear, small toys, books, souvenirs acquired en route, etc.

You should also bring a laundry bag or two and drop them in the bottom of your closet. This will make it easier to organize your clothing and to repack at the end of the trip.

Second, I like to take an over-the-door shoe organizer to hang on the inside of the bathroom door. These also come in a variety of shapes and sizes. I prefer the ones that are clear, sturdy plastic throughout. The plastic ones can more easily be folded up into a variety of shapes and tucked into a spare spot in your suitcase. The transparency of the plastic allows you to quickly see what is in the various pockets at a glance. This item will substantially increase the available storage space in your bathroom and makes it easier to organize your toiletries and the like in an efficient manner. With one of the organizers that have 20 or more generous sized pockets, you can organize numerous bathroom items for each family member – toothbrushes, toothpaste, deodorants, shaving materials, shower caps, lotions, first aid kit, medicines, etc. And, depending on which row is selected, this can make it easier to keep certain items in or out of the reach of small hands.

You should designate a spot for messages – where family members can leave notes as to whereabouts. Because the walls of your cabin will most likely be metal, you can bring and use magnets as a great way to organize materials – messages, swim goggles, cruise lanyards, etc.

Using magnets to organize your cruise card lanyards can be very helpful. Because cruise cards are essential and used so frequently, you will find that most passengers will have the cards secured by or in a lanyard that they can wear around their neck or wrist. You can position your lanyards near the door where they can be easily retrieved. And, you can position them sufficiently high up that they are out of reach of busy hands.

You will also find that you accumulate a great deal of paper throughout the cruise. Indeed, there will likely be papers waiting for you when you first enter your stateroom. There will be daily newsletters about shipboard events, and you will also receive various flyers regarding promotions, shore announcements, or upcoming important events. One magnet can be designated to store all of the old cruise guides and various papers you get while on board. Instead of leaving them strewn about the cabin.

You will also want to bring something to maximize the usability of the electric outlets. There will not be many, and likely only one or two will be readily accessible. A family of four with a variety of tablets, phones, and other devices will need a little help, so pack an outlet expander. One that does not have a surge protector. My favorite is one that has slots for four or five USB connections as well as two plug outlets. It is very compact and takes up minimal counter space.

You may also find numerous items on the counter that you don't really need, or know that you won't use. All of those items can be cleared off and placed in the closet on the high shelf. For instance, I usually clear out the ice bucket and glasses (an unnecessary attractive nuisance for small children) and all of the magazine type items.

All of the organizational items discussed above are readily available at a wide range of retail outlets. For those who would prefer a convenience option over tracking each of these individual items down, most of these items can be purchased as part of a curated collection at www.familycruisekits.com. Purchasers of this book can receive a 15% discount. Please visit http://familycruisecompanion.com/discountoffer for a discount code.

(2) Childproofing your cabin

If you will be traveling with a baby or toddler, you will want to childproof your cabin as soon as you are able to get into your room. Here are some basic tips for childproofing your stateroom:

Check for Overlooked Items
Often the first thing that a toddler does when he or she enters a new space is wander around picking things up; so, ideally, an adult would enter room first to prep.

You should get down on hands and knees and scan the floor for overlooked choking hazards or other hazards. Be sure to look under the bed (lift spread) and in corners of bathroom. Check cabinets and drawers and under desk/vanity. Although all of the staterooms are cleaned prior to a group of new passengers boarding, it is not uncommon for some items to be overlooked, or previously hidden items to go undiscovered. So, for instance, we have often found random pens, coins and such. And once, we found a large bag of small liquor bottles (like the kind you get on an airplane) hidden under the bed.

Clear away unnecessary items in plain view.
Stow magazines and other paper items in a drawer (or wall cubby). Put trash cans up/out of reach. Move glass cups, ice bucket set up, etc., to the top of the closet or otherwise out of reach. If unneeded, ask stateroom attendant to remove. If you have a balcony, move all balcony furniture far from railing. You want to avoid having your kids climbing up and leaning over.

Use duct tape for other hazards.
If you have a mobile toddler with curious, busy hands, you should also consider bringing duct tape or painters' tape. While not absolutely essential, I found it to be quite helpful

when traveling with busy toddlers. You can use tape in the following ways:

- Cover unused outlets
- Fasten washcloth or other cushion to sharp corners
- Secure cabinet doors and/or low drawers
- Secure fridge door (to restrict access to contents and also to prevent tip overs from pulling up or on handle)
- Tape over bathroom door lock, so child cannot lock self inside

D. Mandatory Muster Drill

On your first evening aboard the ship, there will be a mandatory safety drill or muster. All passengers are required to attend, and all dining venues and other distractions are shut down. The drill will take place either at your actual muster station or in some central public location. If you fail to turn up at the muster, crewmembers will likely be dispatched to find you, and the other passengers will be annoyed for having their wait unnecessarily extended.

The primary purpose of the drill is to learn the safety and evacuation procedures and receive instruction on donning life jackets. Different cruise lines have used a variety of formats to communicate the required safety information. But it is usually overly long and dry, and it may be repeated in multiple languages. Bring something to keep your children entertained and reasonably compliant.

CHAPTER 7

ON BOARD THE SHIP

A. Establishing A Family Plan
(i) Onboard Expenses

There will be many opportunities for you and your family to spend money while on board. And, as previously noted, one of the more convenient aspects of cruising is the ubiquitous cruise card. Basically, this allows you to use your room key card as an ID and a charge card to charge all on board charges to your room. You should be advised that kids' key cards also have the ability to charge to the room – so for instance, purchasing game credits at an arcade, candy, snacks, toys at an onboard shop, premium ice cream. The purchase option can be turned on or off. Cruise lines differ on whether the default setting when the cards are issued is at on or off. So you should confirm that as soon as you receive the cards. Some cruises also allow you to set an allowance or spending cap. But regardless, if you intend to allow spending privileges, you should have a talk about limits and expectations. Basically, your child will be running around with a copy of your credit card. So, for instance, you should specifically discuss whether your child is allowed to pay for items for other kids – new friends – on board. I have often seen or heard of kids running up sizable bills in the arcade or candy shop treating their new friends that they made on board.

(2) Communication

Assuming that you are not going to spend 100% of your time with all family members traveling the ship in a pack, you should work out some method of communicating on-board. You should consider working out a schedule at the beginning of the day (perhaps by highlighting a cruise planner), and then have pre-arranged meeting times and places – whether for meals or simple check-ins. You could also plan on one joint activity where everyone meets up. You should have an identified spot in the room to use as a message center so that people can easily leave notes.

A few thoughts on some electronic communication options:

- **Texting** – It can be challenging to use your regular data service for exchanging text messages. Depending on your geography, your cell phone provider may not have coverage. And, even if coverage is offered, it will likely be pricey.

- **Walkie Talkies** – often better in theory than in execution. Such devices can be bulky, burdensome, and hard to hear in some locations.

- **Wi-Fi Apps** – If you have the option to purchase some type of onboard internet/Wi-Fi package, you can communicate using a convenient app. A commonly available one that usually works is *WhatsApp*. It is free to download, and, as of this writing, there is no charge for individual messages. Some cruise lines offer dedicated apps that may have messaging features for a fee. Regardless of whether you use a third-party app or the ship's app, you should be aware, however, that internet coverage is not 100% reliable when you are out at sea. There may be stretches of time when the ship will be unable to get a signal.

B. Internet Access

All major cruise lines offer some type of wireless internet service that you can access using your own personal computers or electronic devices, as well as public shared computers. Most lines offer various tiers of service at different price points – e.g., a fixed number of minutes for e-mail only; unlimited streaming for a daily price; and packages that cover multiple people and/or multiple devices. These packages are often somewhat expensive, but you should look for discount opportunities. For instance, there may be discounted packages available to those who pre-register online (and pre-pay), discounts for first day purchases, or internet access may be offered as a booking promotion.

C. Dining - dining room, specialty dining

You will never have to go hungry on a cruise. All of your basic meals will be included in your cruise fare. The dining options that will not incur any additional charges will be, at a minimum, the buffet and the main dining room. You may also have access to room service at no charge, but the menu will be much smaller, and there may be a surcharge for orders placed after midnight. (*Note that the "free" room service option may soon be changing. At least one cruise line has recently announced their intent to apply charges to daytime orders as well.*)

For the main dining room, you will likely have the option of a "fixed seating" – meaning you sit at the same table every night at a set time and you have the same wait staff; or, you may have an option for flexible or freestyle dining where you can pick your own time for dining, and you can select different venues. Depending on the size of your travel party, your group may be sharing a table with another party.

On my first cruise, which consisted of a party of three single women, we had fixed seating for dinner. Our group of three was assigned to a table that also had a family of 5 from Australia. Before arriving at our numbered table and seeing people already seated there, I had no idea that was how the dining room worked. (These days, there are many alternatives if you do not want to meet new people over dinner.) Although that may not have been my first choice originally, the shared table turned out to be an additional element of fun to our vacation. Our Australian dinner companions consisted of a set of parents traveling with their infant son and his grandparents. They had been traveling in the USA for the past 5-6 weeks and were wrapping things up with a cruise of the Caribbean before heading back home. They had many entertaining stories to share about their travels and life in Australia.

In addition to the buffet and main dining room, there will be other dining venues that assess a flat fee for dining there. These are considered premium dining experiences at specialty restaurants. Representative examples of such restaurants would include a steakhouse, upscale sushi, upscale Italian/French/Fusion, etc. You will be assessed an up-charge for specialty restaurant venues. When I first started cruising, the surcharges were nominal – $5 to $10 per person. Now they are routinely $25 to $30, and I have seen some as high as $50/$75. This can be an area where you use your promotional ship credit or special travel agent promotion. You should also look for discounted packages booking online in advance. Also, they sometimes offer discounted specialty dining packages on embarkation day.

D. Dress Guidelines

Your cruise will have some basic guidelines for appropriate dress in the dining room and similar facilities. Typically, for dinner, this will be some version of nice casual (no swimsuits, ripped jeans, etc.). There will also be one or two evenings that are designated as formal nights. Do not be intimidated. For better or worse, cruise lines have become way more flexible as to what is appropriate dress for formal night. This is a nice opportunity for dress up family pictures. But if you really want to skip it, there are usually other venues on the ship where you can still be casual – e.g., the buffet.

E. Physical activities - rock climbing, pools, ice skating

Virtually every major cruise ship will have a pool and something that passes for a jogging track or walking track. You will also find a gym or exercise room with various levels of sophistication. After these basics, many ships offer a wide range of activities such as rock climbing, ice skating, flight or surf simulators, water parks, and other novelty items.

Please note that many of these activities will come with some type of restriction. For instance, on most ships, swim diapers are not permitted – but there may be a designated pool that allows them or a splash park area. Some activities may require advance waivers and/or have age or height restrictions. Some may also have extra charges.

If there is some activity that you really want to do, you should try to fit it in during the early part of your cruise. As the days progress, the lines for popular activities will grow, and/or activities may be canceled due to weather reasons or technology issues. Also, some activities may only be available at certain scheduled times on specific days and not readily available later in your cruise – e.g., ice skating, bumper cars.

F. Other Entertainment and Recreation

You should not worry about being bored while on the ship. Each day you will receive a cruise newsletter that will include a daily schedule of events and activities taking place on-board the next day. Activities such as bingo, game show-style competitions, dance lessons, movies, and various educational workshops or demonstrations. There will also be some type of evening entertainment – such as a comedian, musical revue, acrobats, or Broadway show. Most of these will not incur any additional charge, but may require advance reservation.

Although the specifics vary by cruise line and among ships within different lines, you will also likely find access to a game room/card room (stocked with popular board games and cards); a library and/or computer center; and some type of sports area with athletic courts and ball equipment.

CHAPTER 8

CHILDCARE ISSUES

One of the most attractive features of family cruising is the ready availability of trustworthy childcare. Thus, you can design a vacation schedule with whatever mix of family time, couples time, adult time, solo time that you prefer. As an added bonus, your kids may be extremely happy to allow you to skip off to your adult activities while they have fun with kids their own age.

In my view, the defining characteristic of whether a cruise is truly "family friendly" is the breadth and depth of its children's programming. Generally, there are three categories of programming – port days, sea days, and evening care options. For cruises that involve a stop at a private island, that will present an additional option to consider.

Most big ship lines offer group babysitting in the kids' club until midnight or later. "Camp" activities tend to be free during the day and early evening, but late-night drop-off playtime usually incurs an hourly cost. Very few lines offer in-cabin babysitting. For those that do, it tends to be based on staff availability, and children often must be one year or older. In addition, cruise lines differ as to whether you can drop off your kids at the club on a port day and then leave the ship. Some require at least one parent or guardian to remain on board if the children are at the kids' club.

A. Kids' Club

The *Kids' Club* will usually be the hub of all youth programming for the ship. Every cruise line will have its own name for the club and different names for groups of children based on ages. Programming during the day is usually provided at no additional charge.

You should expect some type of open house function at kids' club on embarkation day. You should go to check out the facilities and register. During registration, you will inform the staff about allergies or special issues, and decide on who is allowed to drop off and pick up your child. This will be an opportunity to see/tour the facilities, meet the counselors/youth program staff and scope out some of the other kids. There should also be a schedule of activities for the next day. Every night of your cruise, if you register, you should expect to receive a program of events/activities for the youth program for the following day. These are also readily available for pick up at the club.

With the exception of the *Disney Cruise Line*, children will be assigned to different groups based on their age as of the day of embarkation. Most cruise lines will say that these age cut-offs are strictly enforced, but in practice, there seems to be some wiggle room. If your child is close to the cut-off for the next age group and there are clearly understandable reasons why you want to switch groups—you should try talking to the manager. Situations where I have seen some willingness to be flexible – siblings who want to be in the same group and the younger one is relatively close to the cut-off; friends and family traveling together where a younger child is traveling with older companion; children who celebrate birthdays mid-cruise. Obviously, this is case by case; however, they seem willing to at least give it a trial. As long as the child acts consistent with the maturity level expected of kids in that age group, there is usually not a problem.

You should be aware that during slow (off-peak) times, some age groups will be combined. This often happens on port days and/or around lunchtime.

B. Tweens & Independence

If your child is in the 9-12-year-old range, you will likely have the opportunity to allow him some independence and allow him to sign himself in and out of the club. This is entirely your option. Depending on the cruise line, there are typically some limitations on signing privileges. For instance, not allowing children to sign themselves out on port days, or not allowing children to sign themselves out at night after a certain time. You will need to decide how much freedom to roam you will be allowing your child.

One alternative is to allow your child the ability to sign himself in but not out. There is some convenience element to this approach for both the adults and children. So, for instance, if child finishes dinner early and wants to go up to the club, he can easily be dispatched rather than waiting for an adult escort.

C. Options for Infants & Toddlers

Most cruise lines start their regular children's programming at age 3. *Carnival* starts at age 2. These daytime kids' club activities and drop-off services will not incur an additional charge. There is a growing trend of some larger lines to offer paid options for younger children. This is usually at some reasonable hourly fee. Sometimes there are nominal caps on the number of hours a day, and some ships will have reservations.

The following cruise lines currently offer full infant/toddler care on at least some of their ships: *Disney* (starting at 6 months); *Royal Caribbean* (some ships including *Oasis*-class and *Quantum*-class; 6 months); *NCL* (some ships; 6 months). *Celebrity* has an in-room babysitting option for children starting at age 12 months. *Carnival* offers group evening babysitting for infants and children six months and older, and it offers additional infant babysitting on port days during certain prescribed hours.

Some cruise lines will add a gratuity to the nursery bill that you sign after each session. But this is not uniform. If you find that you consistently use the nursery services, you should consider providing a gratuity to the staff at the end of your trip. It is not mandatory, but very much appreciated.

Also, many ships will offer some type of toy lending program. Take advantage of it. Typically, there is a selection of individual toys or packages of toys that can be checked out during your cruise and returned by the last day. No charge. This is a great option for quiet play in your stateroom. Or when you need a new distraction while getting ready for dinner.

D. Summary of Youth Programs for Major Domestic Cruise Lines

Set forth below (in alphabetical order), you will find a summary overview of the key features of the various on-board childcare options for each of the major domestic cruise lines with extensive family and youth programming. You can use this information to assist you in selecting a cruise, and it will also be helpful for planning your time on board the ship.

(If you would like information about the youth policies and programs (or lack thereof) for more than 50 cruise lines, including luxury cruise lines, international cruise lines, and major river cruise lines, download the *Family Cruise Companion's Reference Guide on Cruise Line Youth Programs.* Please visit *http://familycruisecompanion.com/ free-youth-summary* to get your free copy.)

(i) Carnival
(a) Main Kids' Club

Carnival offers three main programs: *Camp Ocean/Camp Carnival* for children ages 2 through 11; *Circle "C"* for younger teens age 12 to 14; and *Club O2* for older teens ages 15 to 17.

Camp Ocean/Camp Carnival – The availability of *Camp Ocean* vs. *Camp Carnival* varies by ship. For both programs, the activities are structured across three age brackets: 2-year-olds to 5-year-olds; 6-year-olds to 8-year-olds; and 9-year olds to 11-year-olds. There are a variety of age-based supervised activities.

Unlike most other cruise lines, *Carnival* does not require that children be potty-trained to participate in youth program activities; however, parents must provide their own diapers and supplies. Staff will not change children over the age of 3. If necessary, parents will be provided a cell phone, and they will be called to come and make the change. Complimentary cell phones will be made available to parents when needed for use on-board the ship only.

All children must be toilet trained for pool and water areas; no diapers or swim diapers.

Circle "C" – This is a designated area for youth ages 12 to 14. On its website, *Carnival* describes this as a place where young teens can hang out, meet new friends, and "enjoy some pretty awesome activities like dance parties, games, outdoor movies and more, in the special Circle "C" area or around the ship. It's all supervised by friendly and fun-loving counselors who want your young teens to have "the best vacation ever." *Carnival* also sponsors special shore excursions for both of its teen groups. Teens must be registered with *Circle C* to participate in activities, but they are free to come and go as they please (i.e., no parental signatures required).

Club O2 – This is a designated area for older teens. According to *Carnival*, this is an area where the older teens can: "Hang out and do stuff like watch movies, listen to music from this decade, play sports and video games, join karaoke jam sessions … maybe even have a pool party or two, all with other high schoolers ages of 15 to 17." *Carnival* has also set up teen-only shore excursions so that these passengers can enjoy the ports with their peers.

(b) Options for Kids Under 3

On *Carnival*, the regular youth programming starts at age 2. See above. No children under the age of 2 will be permitted to participate in *Camp Ocean* or *Camp Carnival* activities (unless they will be turning 2 while on the cruise).

There are specific times on board each ship when children under 2 are permitted to use the camp ocean/carnival facilities. Hours may vary based on itinerary. Generally, on sea days, children under 2 can use the camp facilities from 8:00 a.m. to 10:00 a.m. During this period, parents can stay with their children and use the facilities at no charge. Alternatively, parents may drop their child for an hourly fee ($6.75 plus 15% gratuity). On Port Days, infants may be dropped off with staff starting 15 minutes before the first tour until noon (or from 1:00 p.m. until 5:00 p.m. for ships arriving in the afternoon). The same hourly fee applies. There is no option for a parent to remain in the facility to play with a child during this period.

There is also a fee-based nighttime option for younger infants and toddlers. *Carnival* offers "night owl" group babysitting that starts at age 6 months.

(c) Options in port

Parents may leave children in the care of youth services while they leave the ship. However, they must leave tour information in case of emergency. Note that children ages 16 or older will be permitted to disembark in port without a parent or guardian. A parent can contact the security department to raise this age limit if they prefer.

(d) Options after hours

Carnival offers evening group babysitting programs for kids 6 months to 11 years each evening from 10p.m. until 3:00 a.m. Babysitting services are provided in the form of a slumber party where the kids watch movies and cartoons. Pillows, blankets, and cribs will be provided as needed.

For children ages 9 to 11, *Carnival* also offers an intermediate evening program that runs from 10pm until midnight.

During this time, the youth staff will provide and coordinate various activities. At midnight, this group is folded into the general slumber party group. All children must be registered in advance for the evening babysitting. Parents should note that, unlike during the day hours, the older children (9-11) will not be permitted to sign themselves out. A parent or guardian must pick up all children. The charge for this night babysitting service is $6.75/hr. plus a 15% gratuity, per child. For children in diapers, parents must supply their own diapers and wipes, but the youth staff will change them.

(e) In-room options

Carnival does not offer in-room babysitting services.

(f) Other family activities on-board

Carnival offers a variety of activities across its ships. Some notable highlights:

SkyRide – an elevated bike ride on a two-lane suspended course in pedal-powered go-mobile. Available on newest ship(s) – *Vista*.

Seuss at Sea – An opportunity for families to experience the fantastical world of Dr. Seuss come to life, including well-known characters such as the Cat in the Hat, Horton, and Thing 1 and Thing 1. Typical activities include character parades, interactive story time, arts and crafts activities, and a character breakfast. This program is available on all ships.

Hasbro, The Game Show – giant life-sized versions of Hasbro games (e.g., *Connect 4* and *Yahtzee*) played onstage in game show competition format. Friends and family form teams to compete for prizes.

WaterWorks - onboard water park. Configurations vary by ship.

Other fun family friendly activities include IMAX, SportsSquare, ZSpa, Thrill Theater, Dive-In Movies, and Miniature Golf.

(g) Special character tie-in promotions

Carnival offers several promotions related to Dr. Seuss characters: a *Green Eggs and Ham* Breakfast; Seuss-a-palooza Story Time; and Dr. Seuss Bookville

(h) Other points of note

Carnival provides single and double strollers for rent. These may be used on or off the ship. *Carnival* does not, however, carry any baby food, formula, diapers or other baby supplies onboard its ships.

(2) Celebrity
(a) Kids' Club General

The regular club, known as *Fun Factory*, is open from 9am to 10pm every day. All activities are complementary with the exception of port day meal times.

The *Fun Factory* provides programming for children ages 3-11 across three groups: Shipmates (3-5); Cadets (6-8); Ensigns (9-11). Children who are old enough for the Ensign program are eligible to sign themselves out during regular club hours (9am to 10pm) unless a parent informs the club that sign out privileges should not be authorized. After 10 p.m., an adult must sign out all children, including Ensigns.

Celebrity also offers the X-Club for teens and young adults. X-Club provides supervised activities hosted by youth counselors, including social activities, gaming consoles, sports activities, and late-night teens-only dances.

(b) Options for Kids Under 3
Celebrity does not offer drop-off care for children under the age of 3. The ships will, however, offer designated Toddler Time. This is essentially a facilitated playdate that allows parents and toddlers to interact with children their own age. Suitable toys are provided.

(c) Options in port
Parents may leave their children onboard at kids' club when in port for shore excursions. However, there may be an additional charge of $6 per hour.

(d) Options after hours
After 10 p.m., Celebrity offers group sitting in the kids' club facilities from 10 p.m. to 1 a.m. for a fee. This is called the "slumber party."

(e) In-room options
Celebrity also offers in-room babysitting for a fee of $19/hour for up to 3 children from the same family. In-room sitting is

subject to availability. Children must be 12months or older. 24-hour advance notice is required.

(f) Other family activities on-board

Summer Camp at Sea - Opportunity for children and parents to be introduced to the history, culture, and flavors of the Caribbean through a roster of shore excursions geared toward family fun.

Explorer Academy – Participants engage in various STEM activities.

Creation Station – An art program where children and their families can express themselves. Participants make various artistic creations and have the opportunity to turn them into stuffed keepsakes (for an additional fee).

iTake – A half-day video project where kids create films on board using GoPro cameras. Participants learn to storyboard, film, and edit.

Xbox Program – *Celebrity* offers expansive Xbox facilities and related programing. This program includes dedicated Xbox gameplay stations and mobile consoles for one of the largest game experiences at sea.

Celebrity also offers organized sports competitions and family scavenger hunts.

(g) Special character tie-in promotions

None.

(h) Other points of note

Baby food can be made available at no additional charge, but you must place an advanced order. Allow at least 40 days for Caribbean and Alaska itineraries and at least 80 days for other itineraries. *Celebrity* has an Autism Friendly certification from *Autism on the Seas*. *Autism on the Seas* (AOTS) is a national organization that provides cruise vacation services to accommodate adults and families living with children with Special Needs, including, but not limited to, Autism, Asperger Syndrome, Down Syndrome, Tourette Syndrome, Cerebral Palsy and all Cognitive, Intellectual and Developmental Disabilities.

AOTS has developed an "Autism Friendly Certification Standard" designed for cruise lines to ensure that pre-cruise and onboard services, venues, and amenities are accessible for inclusion and participation by the autism and developmental disability community. The AOTS organization provides training development for Youth Staff and other Shipboard Staff customized to each cruise line and is included as part of the Certification process. For more information about *Autism on the Seas* and services they provide to individual families, please visit www.autismontheseas.com.

(3) Disney
(a) Kids' Club General

Disney organizes its main kids' club differently than other lines. The main club is divided into *Oceaneer Club* and *Oceaneer Lab*, and both are open to children ages 3 to 12. *Disney* does not otherwise separate children based on age. Rather, activity participation is based on a child's interest level and maturity. This allows siblings and friends to play together. Some activities will have recommended ages.

Elaine M. Warren

Oceaneer Club/Lab – In *Oceaneer Club*, children interact with *Disney* characters in various themed magical lands that vary based on the ship (e.g., Andy's Room from *Toy Story*; Pixie Hollow from *Peter Pan*; Millennium Falcon from *Star Wars*). *Oceaneer Lab* provides more learning oriented activities. Both the *Club* and the *Lab* are physically connected, so kids have the ability to move freely between the two sections. This program is open from 9am to midnight. Parents can also receive a pager.

Edge – For tweens, children ages 11 – 14, *Disney* provides an activity center called Edge. *Edge* features a large array of hi-tech entertainment, including an illuminated dance floor and tables with notebook computers for playing games or for accessing a proprietary onboard social media application. There is some overlap in age groups between the *Oceaneer* areas and *Edge*.

Vibe – For teenagers ages 14-17, *Disney* also offers a chaperoned lounge for teens to hang out. *Disney* packs this teen hotspot with music, movies, video games, big-screen plasma TVs, a lounge area, dance floor, Internet café, and teen-only activities into the wee hours. Again, there is a small overlap between the ages covered by *Edge* and the ages covered by *Vibe*.

(b) Options for Kids Under 3

For infants and toddlers, *Disney* offers *It's a Small World Nursery* or the *Flounder's Reef Nursery* (the name varies by ship). The nursery provides drop-off care for children ages 6 months to 3 years. The nursery includes a separate quiet nap area complete with cribs. Space is limited, so advance reservations are required. The nursery charge is $9/hour.

(c) Options in port
You may leave your children in the kids' club when you go ashore on port days. Inform the counselors in the clubs that you will be leaving the ship, and leave a cell phone number and your tour information.

(d) Options after hours
Disney does not offer any after-hours childcare once the main clubs close. Youth clubs stay open until midnight or 1:00 a.m. Nursery is open until 11pm.

(e) In-room options
None.

(f) Other family activities on-board
Bibbidy Bobbidi Boutique – The *Boutique* is owned by Cinderella's Fairy Godmother and operated by her skilled apprentices. It a magical beauty salon where aspiring princesses and knights can make their storybook dreams come true. This is the ultimate in dress-up fantasy. Guests receive the royal treatment with hairstyling, makeup, costumes and more, applied by your very own Fairy Godmother-in-training.

The Pirates League – On certain swashbuckling nights, *Bibbidi Bobbidi Boutique* becomes the place to prepare for the pirate life! Boys, girls, and even grownups are invited to drop anchor and transform into a Caribbean sea dog.

D LOUNGE – *Disney* offers a special lounge designed for families. Parents and children can sing, dance, play games, and enjoy live entertainment together.

(g) *Special character tie-in promotions*

Character Experiences – *Disney* offers a wide range of character experiences throughout its ships. These are opportunities to meet and interact with a variety of your favorite characters from numerous Disney films. Some of the structured experiences include photo ops with favorite characters, designated meet and greet locations for specific characters, a royal tea party with Disney princesses, a meet-and-greet with the Disney princesses, character breakfasts, and special character greeting with the stars of *Frozen*. Some events require reservations.

Star Wars Day at Sea – Select Caribbean cruises from January through April 2017 will feature a designated *Star Wars Day*. Passengers will be able to immerse in the *Star Wars* galaxy as roaming characters patrol the ship, including Imperial Officers, Storm troopers, and *Star Wars* celebrities. These cruises will feature a variety of *Star Wars* themed programs and activities including Jedi training school.

Marvel Day at Sea – On certain designated sailings of the *Disney Magic*, guests can enjoy Marvel Day where they can meet favorite superheroes and participate in all-day themed entertainment. The Marvel Day sailings will feature exclusive action-packed activities, including special opportunities to interact with Marvel heroes and villains, and Marvel-themed youth activities in the *Marvel's Avengers Academy.*

(h) Other points of note

Disney offers a wide range of complimentary baby gear available on board its ships, including diaper disposal units, bottle warmers, bottle sterilizers, cribs and playpens, and strollers. You also have the option to order and purchase certain baby items in advance of your cruise and have them delivered directly to your stateroom. These include items such as diapers, wipes, formula, bottles, food, and bathing supplies. Once onboard, you may also purchase baby supplies from the shops, including diapers, training pants, rash cream, infant formula (ready to feed), bottles, pacifiers, baby food, baby shampoo, baby lotion, and baby powder.

(4) Holland America
(a) Kids' Club General

HAL offers three programs for youth ages 3 to 17. *Club HAL* – Kids' club is offered for ages 3 to 6. No diapers or pull-ups permitted. No assistance in the restroom will be provided. *Club HAL Tweens* covers children ages 7 to 12.

The Loft is available for Teens ages 13 to 17. Note that *Club HAL* has an open door policy, and participants may come and go as they please (children under 12 must be signed in and out). All activities are supervised, but the program director will not be responsible for guests that choose to leave an activity.

On sea days, the *Kids and Tweens* program will be closed between 11:30 a.m. and 1:00 p.m., and between 4:00 p.m. and 7:00 p.m. On port days, these programs will be closed between 4:00 p.m. and 7:00 p.m. On sea days, the *Loft* will be closed between noon and 2:00 p.m., and between 6:00 p.m. and 8:00 p.m. On port days between 8:00 a.m. and 4:00 p.m., the Loft is open, but will not be hosted. It will re-open for hosted activities between 8:00 p.m. and midnight.

HAL also sponsors a youth-oriented *Culinary Arts Center* – Hands-on cooking classes for kids and teens. Two groups: 3-7 and 8-15. Kids will learn basic cooking techniques, kitchen safety, new ingredients, and how to follow recipe instructions.

(b) Options for Kids Under 3
None.

(c) Options in port
Supervised kids program for Kids and Tweens; no hosted events for Teens but space open.

(d) Options after hours
For children ages 3-12, *HAL* offers *Club HAL After Hours* from 10:00 p.m. until 12:00 a.m. The fee is $5 per hour.

(e) In-room options
Limited babysitting services, for children aged 5 and under, are available through the Front Office for a fee of $10 per hour for the first child and $7 per hour for each additional

child. Staff members participate on a volunteer basis and service is not always available. No babysitting services are offered while ship is in port.

(f) Other family activities on-board
America's Test Kitchen – an array of on-board cooking shows and workshops.

BBC Earth Experiences – HAL-exclusive natural history programming that includes concerts, films, shows, and children's activities.

(g) Special character tie-in promotions
None.

(h) Other points of note
Baby food and a limited number of high chairs, boosters, and cribs are available onboard. Items must be requested in advance. *Holland America* also offers diapers, wipes, formula, and baby food for advanced purchase. Orders should be placed at least 90 days prior to sailing. Child-friendly birthday parties can be arranged with advance notice.

(5) Norwegian/NCL
(a) Kids' Club General
NCL offers the *Splash Academy*, which is a drop-off program for children ages 3-12. The children are grouped by age as follows: *Turtles* are 3-5; *Seals* are 6-9, and *Dolphins* are 10-12. Children who are still in diapers will be permitted

to participate in *Splash Academy*, but a parent or guardian must be on standby to change diapers. A special pager/phone will be provided for that purpose. Dolphins can have sign out privileges with parent authorization. In addition to the types of activities that you will usually find in youth programs, *NCL* also offers some activities based on learning circus skills.

Entourage is a teen space for kids 13-17 that combines a hangout zone, dance zone, game zone, and party zone. Program counselors host teen activities and challenges around the ship. Although the program and activities are supervised, some teen centers are used as a hangout when the program is not in session (*e.g.*, sponsored activities are taking place elsewhere on the ship), and those spaces may not be directly supervised at that time. But they will be under surveillance.

(b) Options for Kids Under 3
The *Norwegian Escape* offers drop-off care for children 6 months to 3 years. On other ships, there is "open play" in the *Guppies* playroom and *Guppies Hosted Activities*, but these are not drop-off programs.

(c) Options in port
Generally, parents can leave kids at the club while at port. But in some circumstances, one parent must remain on board with pager (diapers; special needs).

Sign out authorizations do not apply on port days (for 10-12).

(d) *Options after hours*
Late Night Fun Zone runs from 10:30p.m to 1:30 a.m. for children ages 3-12. The fee is $6 per child per hour; $4 per sibling/per hour. (Age 10-12 sign out authorizations do not apply at night.)

(e) *In-room options*
None.

(f) *Other family activities on-board*
Family activities include: Multi-story waterslides, rock climbing wall, miniature golf (*Breakaway & Breakaway* plus class), and *Cirque Dreams* (*Norwegian Epic*). Ship staff also host family-oriented activities such as game shows, sports challenges, pizza making, and trivia contests.

(g) *Special character tie-in promotions*
Previously *NCL* had a promotion with *Nickelodeon* that featured *Nickelodeon* characters. That program ended and has not yet been replaced.

(h) *Other points of note*
Kids who are in diapers or pull-ups can still participate in regular youth club. A parent will be a given pager and must report within 15 minutes to make any necessary changes. If child is in diapers, one parent must remain on board when ship in port to respond to pages. Failure to respond to pages within the required time frame will result in monetary penalties and dismissal from the program.

Some ships have circus school.

(6) Princess
(a) **Kids' Club General**

Princess has recently announced a fleet-wide redesign of its youth program. This includes new programming and a physical redesign of the youth spaces. These new programs will be based on a partnership with *Discovery Communications*, and the space redesigns will be rolled out to individual ships from 2017 through 2019.

Princess now offers *Camp Discovery* for children ages 3-12. *Camp Discovery* offers two rather than three age groupings: *The Tree House* (formerly *Pelicans*) for ages 3-7 and *The Lodge* (formerly *Shockwaves*) for ages 8-12. Parents may authorize self-sign out privileges for ages 8-12. (This appears to be the youngest sign out threshold of the major lines. Most of the other cruise lines do not have self-sign out privileges until ages 9 or 10.)

Princess also offers a supervised *Teen Lounge* for guests ages 13-17, *The Beach House* (formerly *Remix*). Kids sailing on the *Grand and Golden Princess* will also enjoy their own deck space with a *Whale's Tail* splash pool, and teens have a separate hot tub and deck area just for them.

Princess allows parents to join their children at the youth center during activities. Most other cruise lines have policies that do not permit adults into the kids' club facilities during regular programming, with some exceptions made for children with special needs.

(b) Options for Kids Under 3

Kids under the age of 3 can play in the youth center if accompanied and supervised by a parent or caregiver. There is no drop-off care available.

(c) Options in port

Camp Discovery is available at no additional charge.

(d) Options after hours

Princess offers late night group babysitting from 10 p.m. until 1 a.m. The charge is $5 per hour.

(e) In-room options

None.

(f) Other family activities on-board

Organized family activities include family movie nights, carnivals, dance parties, family game nights, and game shows. Families can also enjoy various sporting and recreational pursuits including a golf driving range and miniature golf putting course and ping pong.

(g) Special character tie-in promotions

None.

(h) Other points of note

Children must be toilet trained to use any pools or hot tubs. No diapers allowed.

A limited supply of diapers is available for sale through the on-board boutiques. It is recommended that parents bring their own diapers and wipes. Baby food is available at no additional charge. Requests should be made at least 35 days prior to sailing.

Parents may be issued a pager and must return to the center if a child needs a diaper change, cries continuously, or engages in other unruly conduct. *Princess* reserves the right to remove parents with disruptive kids from the ship.

(7) Royal Caribbean
(a) Kids' Club General

Royal Caribbean offers the *Adventure Ocean Youth Program* for children ages 3 to 11. Children are grouped as follows: *Aquanauts* (ages 3-5); *Explorers* (ages 6-8); *Voyagers* (ages 9 to 11). Parents of 3-year-olds can request pagers. All children must be 100% toilet trained. No diapers or pull-ups are permitted (an exception policy exists for autistic children). In the event of an accident, a parent will be contacted to retrieve the child and make the necessary wardrobe change.

On the *Oasis* class ships, the large dedicated Adventure Ocean space includes activity rooms for each of the designated age groups, the Nursery, a large playroom stocked with toys for open play, a science lab, and a theatre. The theater is used for movies and for performances put on by the children themselves.

Royal Caribbean offers teen programs divided into two groups for guests ages 12 to 14 and guests who are 15 to

17. Teens in the program have the freedom to join in pre-planned activities throughout the day or may choose to hang out in designated teen-only spaces (supervised by *Adventure Ocean* staff). Sample activities for younger teens may include rock climbing competitions, dodge ball, dance activities, movie nights, and talent shows. Older teens may enjoy activities such as pool parties, teen dinners, karaoke competitions, and sports competitions (both virtual and real).

The ships "teen-only" hang out spaces include a low-key lounge area and an evening dance club. *Royal Caribbean* also offers a teen spa on some ships.

(b) Options for Kids Under 3

Royal Caribbean offers several options for children under the age of three. On some ships, there is a dedicated *Royal Babies & Tots Nursery*, which provides drop-off care for infants and toddlers ages 6 to 36 months. Fees apply.

Royal Caribbean also offers organized parent/child activities at designated times (not drop off). There is also an option for in-room sitting for children 12 months or older.

(c) Options in port

Children may be left in the Adventure Ocean club on port days while parents go ashore.

(d) Options after hours

Group sitting is available in Adventure Ocean center for a fee from 10 p.m. to 1:00 a.m. Nursery (some ships) also has evening hours.

Elaine M. Warren

(e) In-room options

Sitters at Sea – for ages 1 and up; sitters bring along toys and games and keep a log of activities. Must be reserved through guest relations at least 24 hours in advance. Sitters assigned on first come first served basis. Service offered between 8:00 a.m. and 2:00 a.m. $19/hr. for up to 3 kids in same family.

(f) Other family activities onboard

Royal Caribbean offers numerous other family-oriented activities and entertainment outside of its *Adventure Ocean Club*.

Pool & Sports deck and other physical adventure activities – water park, rock climbing and rock wall races, table tennis tournament, miniature golf, basketball, *FlowRider* surf simulator, skydiving simulator, ice skating, and roller skating. (Availability varies by ship).

Activities and daily events designed to appeal to family participation - festivals, poolside games, physical challenges, karaoke nights, carousels, zip lines, bumper cars, circus school, and a 3D movie theatre. (Availability varies by ship).

Royal Caribbean also offers family-oriented production shows including puppet shows, ice skating shows, and water shows.

(g) Special character tie-in promotions

Royal Caribbean has a partnership with *DreamWorks* through which it offers the *DreamWorks Experience* on many ships (10 ships at last count), including all of the *Quantum* class and *Oasis* class vessels. The *DreamWorks*

Experience features characters from several *DreamWorks* animated pictures, including – *Shrek, Kung Fu Panda, Madagascar, Trolls, Home,* and more. Activities include character dining, live shows and character parades, 3D movies, and photo opportunities.

(h) Other points of note

Through *Babies 2 Go, Royal Caribbean* offers a pre-order service for diapers, wipes, and baby food that will be delivered to your stateroom at the beginning of the cruise. Play yards must be reserved in advance so that enough will be placed onboard.

Royal Caribbean is a certified Autism friendly cruise line. It provides autism-friendly toys, films, resources, and staff training.

Select *Royal Caribbean* ships have an infant pool known as the *Baby Splash Zone*, where children who wear a swim diaper can go into. Ordinarily, children that wear diapers are prohibited from going into pools onboard the ship, but some of the newer cruise ships now offer an infant pool.

This Chapter has provided detailed information about youth and family programming for the major domestic cruise lines with the most extensive and/or well known offerings. If you would like a summary of the youth policies and programs (or lack thereof) for dozens of other cruise lines, including luxury cruise lines, international cruise lines, and major river cruise lines, please visit *http://familycruisecompanion.com/free-youth-summary* to download your free copy of the *Family Cruise Companion's Reference Guide on Cruise Line Youth Programs.*

CHAPTER 9

HEALTH & SAFETY ISSUES

A. The Infamous Norovirus

One of the commonly expressed concerns regarding cruising is fear of outbreaks of norovirus. You should be aware that norovirus can be contracted anywhere – not just a cruise ship. It is just more attention grabbing when it happens on a ship than in an everyday setting. Also, there are reporting requirements and procedures that result in careful tracking of norovirus episodes on cruise ships.

Fortunately, such outbreaks do not happen often. But, sadly, when they do, they can be quite ugly. The best defense against norovirus is frequent hand washing with soap and hot water. It is the actual rubbing of the hands under running water that washes away the virus. If you have sensitive skin, consider bringing your own hand soap.

You should also bring your own hand sanitizer and use it liberally. Everyone should carry a small pocket size bottle. Hand sanitizer is not a substitute for hand washing but should be used in addition to regular hand washing. To be effective, hand sanitizer should have at least 60% alcohol content. Travel size sanitizer or similar wipes (with high alcohol content) can be particularly useful when traveling on tour buses or visiting ports.

Although every ship will have some type of infirmary or medical center, you should temper your expectations regarding the ship's medical facility. Medical care aboard ship is designed to treat routine illnesses, provide emergency care, and stabilize serious medical problems. They often have very limited and inconvenient hours. They will provide assistance with minor ailments such as constipation and motion sickness. Typically, they will not be in a position to handle any serious health concerns. Those will be referred off-ship. When you purchase travel insurance, procure a policy that includes medical assistance if you must leave the ship. Do expect to be charged for visiting the clinic. In my past experience, these charges were not modest.

B. Safety on ship
Port Safety

When you are visiting a new or unfamiliar port, you should figure out in advance (before leaving the ship) whether there are certain areas of town that should be avoided. This can be researched in advance, but you should also ask the cruise director and/or shore excursion staff. They should be able to provide you with that information or point you to the person who can.

When off-ship, you should always travel with at least one other person. Do not wander around by yourself. Guard against pickpockets. Be mindful of where you keep your valuable items and whether they could be easily accessible to others.

Last, but not least—you should return to the ship on time!

Pool Safety

Most cruise lines do not employ lifeguards, so you should review water safety rules with all members of your family. The only lines that have lifeguards are *Disney* and *Royal Caribbean*. You should make sure that your children take advantage of any available flotation devices (or, alternatively, plan to bring your own). Also, young children should be supervised at all times, even if they know how to swim. It is very easy to run into unexpected trouble in a crowded pool.

Safety on Board

Crime is not common or rampant, but it does happen. Although crimes are not common on cruise ships, you should not be lulled into a sense of false security by being in vacation mode 24/7. Remember that bad apples take vacations, too.

Keep up with your cruise card and report any loss immediately, so that you can be issued a new card. Remember that your cruise card serves a dual purpose – it not only provides access to your room, but it provides access to your cruise charge account. And the same is true for the cruise cards of your children.

Although the ship will have surveillance and security, you should still be cautious of remote/dark areas, and the presence of strangers walking you back to your cabin.

All family members should pay attention during the muster drill. Pay particular attention to the ship's protocol for reuniting children with their parents during an emergency.

Make sure that your children know where to find the guest relations desk. They should also be told to approach the ship's staff on board if they need help. Point out what the uniforms and nametags look like. Also, show them where they can find the house phones (usually by the elevators), and you should figure out what is the ship's procedure for having someone paged in case of emergency.

Instruct children to never go into the stateroom of people who are not in your travel party. This presumptively includes the staterooms of other children (unless you have had the opportunity to meet the other child and his or her family).

If your children have freedom to move independently around the ship, they should keep you apprised of their plans (and let you know if the plans change). You should have some plan for regular check-ins – whether leaving messages in the cabin or meeting up at specified activities at specified times. To the extent your tweens or teens will be walking around the ship in the evening, you should discuss some basic safety rules. For instance, stay with a group. Only drink beverages that you receive directly from a ship server. Do not return to your room unescorted. Do not wander around the ship alone.

CHAPTER 10

PREPARING TO RETURN HOME

A. Settling accounts

At the end of the cruise, you will be provided with a copy of the charges that have been made to your ship account. You will often see a very long line at guest services on the last day as people try to make adjustments or have issues with their bill. To avoid this, you should make a point of getting a copy of your bill midway through the trip to try and catch any problems early.

Please note that most cruise lines have adopted a policy of adding automatic gratuities to your account. This will be reflected as a daily fee assessed for each passenger in your stateroom (including children). These fees generally range from $12 to $18 per day, depending on cabin category, and will be shared among almost all of the ship's service staff. Sometimes the "prepayment" of these automatic gratuities can be selected as a promotional perk at the time you book your cruise. If these gratuities were not paid in advance on your behalf, then they will show up as charges on your ship account. If you do not wish to have your account handled in that manner, you have the option to visit guest services and have adjustments made as you believe appropriate. You also have the option to provide individual cash gratuities to staff members who provided you with exemplary personal service that you would like to recognize—for instance, your stateroom attendant, your assigned table wait staff in the main dining room, a particularly attentive wine steward. This can be in addition to (or in lieu of) the ship-wide gratuities that are automatically assessed. Typically, you will find small envelopes at guest services available for cash tips.

B. Luggage concerns

You will need to have your entire luggage packed up and placed outside your stateroom the last night by a designated time. You will be provided special luggage tags that will have your disembarkation group number. This number controls the time on which you will be allowed to disembark the ship and retrieve your luggage. Your group number assignment is based on whatever travel information you provided at registration. If you need to change your number, you can do so at guest services.

Since you will not have access to your luggage again until after you have left the ship, you need to plan for a disembarkation bag. You will need to leave out whatever sleepwear is needed and your outfit for the next day and required toiletries. You will also need your disembarkation bag to pack up your clothes from the last night, your PJs, toiletries, etc.

C. Ground transportation

You should have a concrete plan for getting from the cruise terminal to the airport. There will be thousands of people disembarking during a relatively short time period, so there can be an extensive wait for cabs. Thus, alternative arrangements are strongly recommended. Even if you don't have to rush and catch a plane, standing in a long taxi line in the heat surrounded by your luggage and small children is not a fun way to end your vacation.

The cruise line will offer a shuttle service (for a fee) that will consist of a large bus. This can be booked while onboard, but you will need to make reservations in advance. You can also arrange for a car service or van service to pick you up and take you to your hotel or the airport. This has been my preferred option – particularly for longer cruises with lots of luggage.

D. Looking Ahead to your Next Cruise

So, if you decide that you enjoy cruising, one of the best times to book your next cruise is while you are still on the ship. There is a special office called "Future Cruises" that will be happy to assist you. There will typically be an enhanced discount or bonus for booking while still onboard. And usually, there is no downside to doing so. You can cancel before final payment deadline, or you can transfer your promotion to a different cruise if you change your mind once on land.

You should also be aware that many land-based loyalty programs offer cruise promotions. So, for instance, if you or a travel companion is a casino player, *MGM* has a partnership with *Royal Caribbean* and *Caesars* has a partnership with *NCL*. Through these programs, it is possible to get heavily discounted and/or free cruises as well as other onboard perks.

E. Closing Thoughts

Hopefully, your cruise will have been absolutely wonderful, but if it was not - don't be afraid to complain. And if you really have something to say, put it in a letter and send it once you are off the ship. If you take the time to actually put your concerns in writing, you will most likely be contacted by a ship representative who will try to make things right.

Many people express some anxiety at the idea of taking a cruise with small children. Don't be intimidated. Just remember, **thousands** of people have already gone before you. I hope my words help pave your way.

I would love to hear from you. Please come share your thoughts and experiences at **www.familycruisecompanion. com**.

TOP 6 THINGS TO KNOW WHEN PLANNING A CRUISE WITH A BABY

- Pack plenty of diapers, wipes, and formula
- Bring your own dish soap and scrub brush
- If possible, have cabin where you can isolate baby/kids for nap – *e.g.*, balcony stateroom
- Assume no bathtub and make plans accordingly
- Nail down options for childcare on your specific ship
- Bring an inexpensive umbrella stroller and leave your deluxe model at home

You can download a copy of the *Family Cruise Prep & Pack Checklist* which contains additional tips and packing suggestions in a handy checklist format. Please visit *http://familycruisecompanion.com/prep-and-pack-list* to get your copy.

TRAVEL INSURANCE

(1) Some Leading Insurance Companies:

- www.allianztravelinsurance.com
- www.AmericanExpress.com/travelinsurance
- www.travelguard.com/travelinsurance
- www.travelexinsurance.com

(2) Some websites comparing travel insurance:

- www.insuremytrip.com
- www.squaremouth.com
- www.tripinsurancestore.com

PLANNING SHORE EXCURSIONS

(1) Websites where you can research options:
www.Tripadvisor.com
www.Cruisecritic.com

(2) Sampling of Tour Operators/Day Passes
Here are some places to start. Please search for recent reviews related to your specific port.

resortforaday.com
bahamasdaypass.com
cozumeldaypasses.com
nassauparadiseisland.com
shoreexcursioneer.com
cruisingexcursions.com
shoreexcursionsgroup.com
cruiseshorexcursionsjamaica.com
shoreexcursionsinitaly.net
alaska-shoreexcursions.com
privateshoretrips.com

(3) Plan to Take a Snack

Be sure to pack snacks for excursions. Some of them can be long and/or you may encounter unexpected delays. Before you disembark, you can stop by the buffet to grab dry cereal, cartons of milk, crackers, rolls, etc. (When my kids were toddlers, they loved sausage; so we always took a little baggie and packed some up.) You should avoid fresh fruit and veggies because there may be restrictions on such items coming off or on the ship.

TOP 6 TIPS FOR MAKING YOUR CABIN MORE COMFORTABLE

- Unpack fully and store empty luggage under the bed.
- Use the closet hangers provided to hang as many clothes as feasible and conserve drawer space.
- Use an over-the-door shoe organizer to expand and organize your bathroom storage space.
- Use a foldable closet organizer and laundry bags to expand storage space and keep order in the family closet.
- Use magnets to turn cabin walls into storage for newsletters, flyers, lanyards and other small items.
- Use an electrical outlet expander to multiply charging options for your family electronics.

Some of the items listed above can be purchased as part of a curated collection at www.familycruisekits.com. Purchasers of this book will receive a 15% discount. Please visit http://familycruisecompanion.com/discountoffer for a discount code.